Real Estate Investing For Beginners
2 Books In 1

How to build a passive income with real estate investments and rents

WILLIAMS W. SCOTTY

© **Copyright 2020 by Williams W. Scotty**
All rights reserved.

This document is geared towards providing exact and reliable information with regards to the topic and issue covered. The publication is sold with the idea that the publisher is not required to render accounting, officially permitted, or otherwise, qualified services. If advice is necessary, legal or professional, a practiced individual in the profession should be ordered.

- From a Declaration of Principles which was accepted and approved equally by a Committee of the American Bar Association and a Committee of Publishers and Associations.

In no way is it legal to reproduce, duplicate, or transmit any part of this document in either electronic means or in printed format. Recording of this publication is strictly prohibited and any storage of this document is not allowed unless with written permission from the publisher. All rights reserved.

The information provided herein is stated to be truthful and consistent, in that any liability, in terms of inattention or otherwise, by any usage or abuse of any policies, processes, or directions contained within is the solitary and utter responsibility of the recipient reader. Under no circumstances will any legal responsibility or blame be held against the publisher for any reparation, damages, or monetary loss due to the information herein, either directly or indirectly.

Respective authors own all copyrights not held by the publisher.

The information herein is offered for informational purposes solely, and is universal as so. The presentation of the information is without contract or any type of guarantee assurance.

The trademarks that are used are without any consent, and the publication of the trademark is without permission or backing by the trademark owner. All trademarks and brands within this book are for clarifying purposes only and are the owned by the owners themselves, not affiliated with this document.

Table Of Contents

RENTAL PROPERTY INVESTING FOR BEGINNERS

Introduction 2

Chapter One 13

Methods Of Buying Rental Properties 13

Chapter Two 25

Choosing The Style Of Investment And Right Property 25

Chapter Three 47

Factors To Consider Before Investing 47

Chapter Four 64

What Tenants Look For In A Rental Property 64

Chapter Five 74

Landlords Guidance For Rental Property Gardens And Outside Spaces 74

Conclusion 81

HOW TO INVEST IN REAL ESTATE

Introduction 86

Chapter One 88

How To Invest In Real Estate Are You Investing Correctly? 88

Chapter Two 100

Best Places To Buy Real Estate 100

Chapter Three 117

Buying Real Estate In Different Countries 117

Chapter Four 134

How To Buy Real Estate Below Market Value 134

Chapter Five 153

Real Estate Mistakes To Avoid 153

Conclusion 162

RENTAL PROPERTY INVESTING FOR BEGINNERS

A guide on how to create income with rental property investments

WILLIAMS W. SCOTTY

INTRODUCTION

When talking about Rental Property Investments, it is necessary to understand the word ' working capital.' Working capital has two concepts: gross working capital and net working capital. The Gross working capital was the total of the current assets. Total working capital was the difference between current assets and current liabilities. Although this working capital concept is commonly used, it can be stated here that It's an economically meaningless accounting concept. There is little point in saying a company's net working capital is managed. What an enterprise is really doing is making decisions on different current assets and liabilities.

Today, as an investor in a rented property, you will need a deep knowledge base to thrive in this demanding real estate and economic environment. The days of easy finance from lenders to purchase investment properties with double-digit annual appreciation have gone by. Business knowledge will "let you know what you're into" to prevent potential problems and unnecessary investment errors. Once applied, practical information is the key to making an intelligent rental investment, which will create a sound financial future for you.

If you think it's that easy to buy and rent a property and collect it, you're really wrong. Looking at it as a way of generating extra incomes, everything looks great because, apart from the income of the renters, you can also benefit from house price increases, which have been ongoing for a few years. There are drawbacks to being a residential owner.

What Is Rental Property Investment?

The term ' working capital' must be understood when talking about rental property investments. Working capital has two concepts: gross working capital and net working capital. The balance of all current assets is the Gross Working Capital. The difference between current assets and current liabilities is net working capital. Although this concept of working capital is commonly used, it is an accounting concept with little economic significance. There is little point in saying that a company manages its net working capital. What a corporation actually does is to agree on various current assets and liabilities.

Working capital management refers to the management of current assets and liabilities. Of course, the main thrust is to manage current assets. This is understandable because, in current assets, current liabilities arise. Working capital is an important facet of investing in rental property since investment in current property accounts for a large share of total investment. In addition, investment in current assets and current liabilities must be quickly oriented towards sales changes. Certainly, fixed asset investment and long-term funding often respond to changes in sales. This relationship is, however, not as close and direct as it is for working capital components.

The importance of managing work capital reflects the fact that financial managers spend a lot of time managing current assets and liabilities. It takes financial managers a great deal of time to organize short-term finance, negotiate favorable credit terms, control the flow of cash, administer receivable accounts, and monitor investment in inventory.

Two attributes of current assets must be taken into account in the allocation of working capital. First, short life span and second, rapid change to other types of properties. Current assets are short-lived. The service life of current assets depends on the time needed for acquisition, production, distribution, and the extent to which they are coordinated.

Rental investment in real estate is an excellent option for investors as they are concerned about sudden slumps and insignificant bursary gains.

Were you looking for investment in rental property? Once you start your search for a home, make sure you know how to be a landlord. Although it is a profitable enterprise, it is by no means a cinch. You will retain the property to reap the financial benefits over the period of ownership.

For many, investment in rental properties is simply a matter of buying a house, renting it, and raking in bucks as they rest on a couch. This is not feasible, however, particularly if you want daily rental income in the coming years. Bagging a rental property and generating a healthy rental income for one year or two is simply an ordinary task. However, it is important for you to keep your rental income steady until you sell the property.

As an investor, nothing is worse than keeping a vacant rental property. This is because you still need funds to maintain the house, which is not returning you as it is empty. You should, therefore, actively search for tenants and do everything you can to keep them happy. It requires attention to the needs of the tenants and prompt maintenance. Although you may be doing some minor repairs yourself, it is best left to a professional to do other difficult tasks (fixing tube leaks and window panels).

In your quest for investment in renting a property, you find the locale key. It includes the distance from the house, the availability of tenants, the average rent that you are able to collect, and the willingness of tenants in the position to pay you. Some locals may be more advantageous than others. For example, it is better to rent a house near a university, because a large number of students are likely to look for a house near their college. This results in a wide range of tenants throughout the year.

For example, the investment in rental property involves analyzing the location, doing whatever it takes to rent your property, keeping your tenants happy, and preserving the property, thus keeping the vacation period to a minimum year after year.

Rental Property Investment - What You Have to Know

Buying a rental property can be a very good investment. If you select the property that is right, tenants can give you a steady income. If you look after the property well or make improvements or if property values increase in the area, you can make a nice profit if you ever resell it. Before investing in a rental property, you should remember other issues.

What you should know about the place

The location of the property may be the most important consideration. When you look for market values in this area, you can determine whether the demand price is fair or how much room there can be for negotiation (almost always some negotiation is possible).

Factors affecting the value of a property include the overall economy of the city, its proximity to highways, main streets, or public transport, the crime rate, and community aesthetics.

What is your contest?

If it's a commercial property, what kind of company do you intend to lease? Is there a rival enterprise, like a new shopping center, that could make these businesses harder?

Find out what other similar properties are paying for rent if it is a residential property. Find out if there are new developments in the research that could compromise the prices to be paid.

Your tenants

Find out a little about them if you keep tenants already on the property. Are they reliable and solvent? If this is a new project and new tenants are to be sought, check local rates so you can carry out a realistic assessment of your future income.

The property

Make sure to examine all relevant aspects of the house, including electric cable quality, plumbing, required structural repairs, parking, and so on. If repairs or other changes are needed, make sure that it is clear whether the seller is taking care of it or not.

If you see the house, some work is done, do not just assume it is finished. The seller could intend to discontinue any further changes following the sale. If the seller wants to make no necessary changes, it can be a point of bargaining to lower the price.

Financing

The best financing option you can obviously find. Sometimes it may be better to find an alternative for the use of your own money even when you have a down payment and have been approved for a loan. This may include various options for innovative funding. Sometimes a distressed seller accepts a note (future payment promise or the IOU) instead of some of the down payment. An investment partner can also be sought.

When making a rental property, there are some of the key points to consider. It's best to know what happens in advance with all facets of the contract, so there are no surprises.

Rental Properties Investment For Beginners

If you are an amateur investor, you have to pay attention to famous investors ' experience and advice. Investing in rental properties for amateurs is, therefore, a crucial step, but at the same time, it is much less costly.

Why is it much less risky than other investment forms?

This is because investing in these particular assets ensures that certain investment returns (ROI) are earned. You may not be able to recover money instantly, but you know that you can raise funds over the long term. It is based on which scheme you should make your first investment.

At the outset, you have to understand the entire investment cycle. Begin to talk to experienced people who have achieved good results. You should ask those who benefit from finding out which way rental property investments benefit.

When you are prepared to cash out, it is the perfect time to search the Internet for rental properties. It could currently or vacantly be held and in good condition. It is, therefore, important to know the state of the property because it determines the quality of the rental.

You don't have to buy a property online and renovate it before you rent it. That'd be very imprudent. Another bonus would be a property with tenants who have contracts. It will bring you immediate profit if the next rent is due.

Types of Rental Properties

If you've been to the market for a home, you know you can choose from various types of housing, including apartment buildings, condominiums, townhouses, and co-operators, besides homes for single families. In this section, we give you an overview of each property and demonstrate how you can make an attractive real estate investment.

In terms of investment, our top suggestions are single family homes and apartment buildings. We do not support the attached housing units in general. If you can buy a smaller single-family house or apartment instead of a common unit, buy the home or apartments for one-family use.

If you can afford a substantial down payment (25% or more) you may be financially challenged by the early years of the property's rental: producing positive cash flow is simpler for all properties because your mortgage costs remain fixed (if you use fixed-rate financing), while rentals rise more quickly than your costs. Regardless of what you purchase, ensure that your rental income and expenditure numbers are run to see whether you can handle the negative cash flow that often occurs in the early years.

Single-family homes

Single-family homes are generally better than detached or shared housing as a property. In a good immovable market, many people appreciate housing, but homes with a single-family tend to surpass other types of housing for the following reasons: single-family houses attract more potential buyers-most people prefer to live separately or independently, particularly for increased privacy, when they can afford it.

Attained or shared housing is cheaper and easier to build and overbuild; this surplus potential means that these properties tend to appreciate their prices more moderately.

Because so many people prefer to live in single-family homes, market prices for such homes can sometimes escalate beyond the limits of rental income generated by these homes. That's exactly what happened in some parts of the US in the mid-2000s and contributed partly to a substantial price correction in the years to come. Compare the monthly cost (after-tax) of owning a house with the monthly rent for this same property to find out if you're buying on this market. Focus on markets where rents are higher than or close to the cost of ownership and shun areas when ownership costs are higher than rents.

Single-family homes with a single occupant are easier to deal with than multi-unit complexes with multiple tenants and units managed and maintained. However, the downside is that a vacancy means that there is no income. Consider the effect of 0 percent occupancy on your estimated income and expense statement for a few months! In comparison, a vacancy in a building with four apartments (each with the same rents) means you still earn 75% of the gross potential (total maximum) rent.

You are responsible for all repairs with a single-family home. You may hire someone to do the job, but you must also locate the contractors and organize and supervise the work. However, understand that if you buy a single home with lots of fine facilities, you may find it harder and harder to have tenants who do not treat it with the same tender love that can be you.

The first rule of success is to release any emotional attachment to a home. But this type of attachment on the part of the tenant is favorable: the more they make your property their home, the more likely it is that they will remain in good health and return it to you, except for the expected normal wear and tear of daily living.

Profiting from the monthly cash flow with a single-family home in the early years is generally the hardest step. The reason: these lands are sold by ally at a premium price compared with their rent (you pay extra for the property you can not rent). Do note that you have no rental income with only one occupant if you have a vacancy.

Attached housing

As land costs have gone up over decades in many areas, packing more housing units attached to a particular plot of land makes housing More accessible. Communal housing makes much sense for developers who are not interested in building security and safety issues.

The investment benefits of three kinds of attached housing, condominiums, townhouses, and co-ops are discussed in this section.

Condos

Condos are typically apartment-style units that are stacked on top or next to each other and sold to individual owners. If you purchase a condominium, you are actually buying the interior of a particular unit as well as an interest in common areas–the pool, tennis courts, courts, hallways, laundry facilities, etc. Although you (and your 10-year-olds) use and enjoy all of the common areas, remember that the householder association actually owns and maintains both the common areas and the structures (typically the foundation, the roof, the storage, electric, and other building systems) themselves.

One of the advantages of a condo as an investment property is that the condos are usually the lowest sustaining assets of all attached housing options because most condominium societies deal with issues such as roofing and planting for the whole structure and profit from the purchased quantity. Please note that you are still responsible for the necessary maintenance within the unit, such as repair equipment, interior painting, etc.

While condos can be easier to maintain, less than single-family homes or apartment buildings are valued if the apartment is not located in a desirable urban area.

Condosminiums may begin in life as condos or apartment complexes, which then become condominiums.

Be careful about apartments transformed into condominiums. While they often constitute the most affordable housing options in many areas of the country and can also be hurt by an excellent urban location that can not be easily re-created, you may have some difficulty with buying. Our understanding is that these transformed apartments are usually old and luxurious (new walls, new appliances, modern landscaping, and fresh paint coat). Be warned: The cosmetic makeover may look good at first glance, but the property probably still has 40 years old electric and plumbing, poor sound insulation, and many economic and functional obsolescence.

In a few years ' time, most owners will move to the traditional family home and rent their condos. You may then find that the property is mainly occupied by renters and have a voluntary board of directors that are unwilling to assess each month in order to maintain the aging structure properly. Such properties may well be the worst in the area within 10 to 15 years of conversion.

Townhomes

Townhomes are mainly attached or house-rooms, a hybrid between a typical airspace condominium and a house with one family. City houses are usually connected, like condominiums, typically sharing walls and a continuous roof. However, city homes are usually two-story buildings that feature a small courtyard and provide more privacy than a condominium because you have no one on top of your building.

Unlike condominiums, you completely have to search the relevant documents before you buy the property to see exactly what you legally possess. City houses will usually be organized as planned unit developments (PUDs) where each owner has fee-simple ownership (no limitation on the transfer of ownership rights-one could have the complete ownership rights) of his individual lot, including his living area and a small area of immediately adjacent territory for a patio or balcony. The common areas are all part of a larger single lot, and the title of each owner is a proportionate proportion of the common area.

Co-ops

Cooperatives are a kind of shared housing with common elements of apartments and condos. You have a stock document that represents your share of the entire building, including the rights to use a particular living space, by a separate written occupancy agreement when buying a cooperative. Unlike a condo, if you wish to renovate or rent your unit to a tenant, you generally need to be approved by the cooperative association. In certain businesses, you even have to seek the permission of the company to sell the device to a prospective buyer.

Turning a co-op into a rental facility is often severely restricted or even forbidden and, where permitted, is typically a hassle because not only the occupant but also the other owners in the building have to accommodate them. Co-ops are also typically considerably harder to fund, and the normal finicky company board approves sales. Therefore, we highly recommend that you reject investment cooperatives.

Apartments

Not only have a healthy long term growth opportunity in apartment buildings, they often have positive cash flow (rental income-expenditure) in the early years of ownership. But like a family home, the buck stops with you to maintain an apartment building. You can employ a property manager to help you, but you still have oversight (and additional costs) duties.

Apartment buildings in the real estate financing world are divided into two groups based on the number of units: four or fewer: better financing options and terms for apartment buildings with four units or fewer because the apartments are considered to be residential properties.

Five or more units: complexes with five or more units are considered a commercial property and do not have very favorable loan conditions for properties with one to four units.

Apartment buildings, in particular more apartment buildings, usually produce a low positive cash flow in the early years rent ownership (unless you are on an overpriced market where it can take 2 to 4 years to break even before tax).).

One way to add value is to turn an apartment building into condominiums if zoning allows. Nonetheless, keep in mind that this metamorphosis requires substantial zoning work and an estimate of restoration and construction costs.

CHAPTER ONE
Methods of Buying Rental Properties

The purchase of rental properties is a good way to increase your property. However, it is challenging to choose the right property. Here are some things to check before you buy a rental property.

1-Place

Most people are unwilling to stay in the boondocks. The location of your accommodation defines how convenient it is to pay. If you have a lot of car traffic, a sign on the web could tell you more than you would from a newspaper.

Locals want to live near all facilities in nice neighborhoods. We want to be close to schools, stores, recreation places, hospitals, and jobs.

I haven't met someone wanting to live in an unwelcome neighborhood or push a gallon of milk for 15 minutes.

2. Numbers

You, want to check the numbers while buying a rental property. Make sure you have all the expenses incurred in this property to ensure that the cash flow is still positive.

Take into account maintenance issues and any facilities not provided by the owner and amortize costs of major projects, such as boiler repair, new roofs, siding, or landscaping.

Such projects only happen once every 15-20 years, but in the 10th year of this period, you can arrive. Please remember to measure high and low expenditures and profits. This can save you a few surprises along the way.

At least one month per year for the unit to be empty due to change. You have to paint the tapestries and clean them for the first two weeks, then print them and exhibit them in the next two weeks. Only 11 months of rent per year should be counted.

3. Lower Maintenance Buildings

Homes that require expensive maintenance are to be avoided. Homes that have shingles or sidings, wooden sides, wooden framework windows, brick entrances, cedar decks, etc., are some examples of this. Take a look down the road and identify future maintenance needs. Remember that less maintenance and higher profits are fewer headaches.

4. Higher Home Prices

Check in higher home prices in cities, because this increases the demand for property rentals. Search for the hideous house on the lower price block, which helps you to buy within the margins.

With a little interior and exterior painting, some light as well as new curtains, a house which will Viola ' receive premium rent for the neighborhood class.

When people can't afford to buy a home, they will have to rent. This creates a demand for land rental.

5. Below market rent prices

Look for rented properties that are below current market rents when you purchase a rental property. It allows you to increase the rent and the value of the property. As stated above, this may only require a little fluff in order to raise the rental price.

The market value of the rental property is determined by the amount of income received from the rental property. But be aware that when you buy the property, renters may not like it when you raise the rent. Check to see what kind of rental is available. The rent is for sale.

If the current renter paid a lower standard price and lived for 1 1/2 years, this could prove to be a losing proposition.

As a new owner, there is only one way to cut a rental short. You have to restructure the spot. Check the local housing commission for the minimum costs for the immediate expulsion of current rental holders. Normally it is only $10,000.00 to restructure costs to get a redeployment. By the way, you haven't told me this!

6. Good rental history

You must check the rental history when you buy properties. Check how long tenants live and pay their rent on time on average. Other areas of the city inevitably have high turnover times. Near to airports, night clubs, military bases, etc.

7. Comply with Zoning and Fire Codes

Make sure you check to see if inspections for a rental property are required by local officials and this property inspects. You never know why the current owner sells the property.

To carry out the inspections, comprehensive repairs may be necessary. A fast red flag would be if the power was switched off for more than 90 days. You would typically need an inspection before power is restored, particularly if the rental is identified.

8. Less than 20 Years Old

It is self-explanatory; if you restrict your options to buildings under the age of 20, you can minimize the probability that the building will have some building code or maintenance problems.

The building may be near to the roof, paint, and possibly furnace repair process, but the foundation is sound and does not need updated windows, side, or re-work of cement.

9. Of State owners or administrators

Look for properties owned by state owners when you lease rental property. It is difficult to manage a rental property from outside of the state, and when these are rented, owners usually want to sell more quickly than get top dollars.

You have to live nearby in order to rent a place fast so that you can show it at the request of the caller. Often in the next 20 minutes, they inquire to see it. Meet your demands and reveal it easily. Many people need a place in the next week or so and won't wait until next week, because you're busy.

They often decide before taking, when it would be more convenient for you to show it. This has always happened to us.

Never send the drive-by mail. Forward-looking renters will request the address to drive around and just look at the location. Don't waste time with these people. Insist that it be shown in the next 30 minutes, or you will not give the address to neighbors as a courtesy.

10. The community is healthy or better-

Obviously avoids deteriorating neighborhoods, looks at the writing on the walls, and stays away. While these can be nice because of the low purchase prices, rent collection is very difficult.

Having safe or changing neighborhoods makes renting the property easier, and you can increase the rent. The general consensus is that the better the region, the higher the purchase price and the higher rental prices, the greater the profit margin. The poorer the area is, the lower the demand and the lower the rental prices, which higher the profit margins.

Don't be afraid to buy nicer rental spots. People who can afford $1000.00 a month will most probably be able to pay on time, compared to someone who can afford just $350.00 a month. In the latter scenario, you're angry, and if at all, you won't get your rent on time. The rental of high-end spots is far more stable than a slumlord!

Protecting Your Rental Property

If properly done, being a landlord can be very rewarding and quite lucrative. However, you need to be aware of problems with the property and make sure you are not liable for them. You want to be sure that something you thought was an investment and asset does not become your and your family's liability.

You want to ensure that you have insurance, both casualties, and liabilities, on your property. You may need to find a good business insurance company specializing in property rental insurance, and they could point you in the right direction and the costs. Keep in mind that property insurance won't necessarily protect you if someone injures you.

Some insurance will cover you only when your property is involved in some kind of catastrophes like a fire or other damage. Liability will only protect you if you are liable for the losses of another person, such as your tenant. There is something to keep in mind when your property is in an area of floods. Umbrella insurance can also be a good option, protecting you against things that the other two types of insurance won't.

Liability insurance will protect you, whether it is a tenant or employee of yours if someone is injured in your property. It will also cover you if you are usually charged with discrimination. If you have employees working on your house, it's a good idea to make sure each employee has a certificate of insurance or benefits, if you don't.

Always ensure that your policy is reviewed every time it is reviewed. You may only have good intentions to realize that you are not adequately insured. When a disaster strikes in the future, you want to be ready with the right insurance already in place. You may be in a troubled world if something just happens to find out you don't have the insurance to deal with it.

Develop good working relationships with people to help you in your business, such as property lawyers, property brokers, property professionals, and tax professionals. You will make your life much simpler if you have these relationships when you need them. Renting property is regulated by the B law; there are many laws governing how you do business. No excuse for ignoring the law, meet your lawyer and accountant at least once a year to make sure you do everything and do it all properly.

You may need a commercial license to go to the City Hall to find out what your business needs are in your city or city. Sometimes you have to have a license for each property; we only need one in our particular province.

Finally, remember that your property insurance does not cover the property of the renter who lives in your house. It could be a good idea to ask for the tenant to have the insurance of the renter if something happens. The best way to reduce responsibility is to ensure that your property is safe. Let your tenants know that you are allowed to inspect the property according to your needs, be sure that it is in your lease and not after that.

If you are a landlord, it can be very rewarding and very lucrative. But you must hear about problems with the property and be confident that you are not responsible for any of them. You want to make sure something you think is an investment, and an asset does not become a liability for you and your family.

You want to make sure you have covered both catastrophes and liability in your house. You might have to find a good insurance agent specializing in rental property insurance that could point you in the right direction to what you need and how much it costs. Keep in mind that property insurance will not necessarily protect you if somebody is hurt.

Most insurance will cover you only if your property has any type of disasters like a fire or other damage. Liability will only compensate you if you, such as your partner, are liable for the damages of someone else. There is something to be kept in mind when the property is in a flood zone. Umbrella insurance can also be a good option that covers risks; the other two types of insurance will not.

Liability insurance will protect you, whether your property is a tenant or employee, should someone be injured on your property. It also protects you if you are typically sued for discrimination. If you have employees working on your property, it is a good idea to ensure that everyone carries an insurance certificate or workers' compensation, if you don't do so, you may be set to disaster.

Please ensure that each time the strategy is checked. You may only have good intentions to know that you are not properly insured. When a disaster strikes in the future, you want to be armed with the right policies. You could be in a world of trouble if something just happens to discover that you have no insurance.

Develop good working relations with people, including property lawyers, real estate brokers, property professionals, and tax professionals, who will support you in your business. You will make your life much simpler if you have these relationships when you need them. Property rental is regulated by b law, and there are many laws governing the manner in which you do business; you have to understand them. No excuse for ignoring the law, meet your attorney and accountant at least once a year to make sure you comply and do everything correctly.

You may need a business license to go to the city hall and find out what the requirements are in your city or city where you have your rental business. Sometimes you have to have a license for each property, and we only need to have one in our particular county.

Finally, remember that your property insurance will not cover the rental property of the renter who lives in your house. It might be a good idea to have renter's insurance if something happens. The best way to reduce accountability is to ensure that your property is secure. May your tenants know that you have the right to inspect the property as necessary, make sure that it is in your rental and not after the fact.

Finding Houses For Your New Property Business

We looked at market research last time, and one of the topics was properties currently available for rent in your city. These can be found on the websites of your competitor and are listed in the local press. Make a list of all properties in your vicinity. It is an excellent exercise to type and list them in order of price on your word processor. Most agencies are letting property list prices as PCM. That's the price for each calendar month, but prices occur on a weekly basis in some places, especially in and around London. Make sure that you compare prices like with like. In order to see how the agencies list properties in your country, in your area, you must double-check.

As each regular ad appears, enter the new prices in the correct position on your list, first the cheapest and last the most expensive. What's that point? You almost note what a detached bungalow (really priced) might be worth in one area of your town or district or an apartment in another two bedrooms. It's all part of building your knowledge to become the local rental expert. And you will already have a detailed registry to refer to when it comes to determining property for rent for real. It's true that these properties aren't yours, not yet, but you can go to school on these tests, and they will teach you a lot.

But you need properties for yourself, of course, so let's get them. But where will you find them? They're out and waiting for you, trust me, more than ever. Here's where. Where's. 1. Have you or any of your friends or relatives an empty property? Has anyone you know recently passed away? If so, what happened to the building? Do you know of any property that has not been sold and sold for months? Anyone of these can be your first guidance. Reach out with the owners and ask them whether they would like to leave. If a property is empty, it costs money. If it's allowed, it produces money, which is a big difference. And think about it. And think about it. If people inherit property, why are they so hurried to sell? The response is, of course, money, probably never before saw that much cash and can't wait to spend on a world cruise and a German sports car. But what happens when the money is gone in a year or two? They're back to one location. Stoney broke. Stoney broke.

But if the property is leased out, it creates money for good and doesn't depend on the fact that it also increases value over time. You can only sell a house once, rent it indefinitely, and, as with everything else, it will increase over time. If you meet someone who is desperate to sell a home, have a word with them. Point them out. Find them out. Why Sell? Why Sell? To sell people? It's an error. If they're desperate for money, they can always see the bank director and take a loan, but keep the house. It's a cash cow that has always been and will always be.

Second, why not rent the house in which you now live? Who! What! Yeah, I'm serious, don't you want the property? Why don't you begin with your own? Maybe the children have grown up and left home, and now you bounce around in a big house with four bedrooms. Do you need all that space? You probably don't. You probably don't. So why not rent a smaller two-bedroom bungalow and rent your home for a year or two? After all, you don't sell your house, and if you miss it, you can always return when the rental contract expires. And if you rent your own house, make sure you value it highly, so you won't spend that much and hassle because you earn money. Right? Right? Love it, and if you let, you're gaining money, if you don't let it, you lost nothing. I did that twice, and it worked very well for me. But, naturally, we want more, we do. Put on your boots and take a trip around the city. Take a notebook and visit all websites that feature postcard advertising. It could be in the post office, a canteen, a pharmacy, shopping centers, a newsstand, wherever you can find little commercials. Properties mentioned there are usually found. On a good day, two or three can be on each platform. Taking the information and the telephone numbers in particular and get ready. These properties are, of course, not yours, but they could be with a little effort. How? How? Of course, by ringing the owners.

Cold telephone calls are not easy and should only be made if you feel best. Take a few copies of what you have to say before calling anyone because we can dry up at the moment's spur. Ring them up and smile. Smile. You don't have to see a person know whether they smile, you can hear it in their voice, and do we, not all, prefer to deal with happy people that are attractive? Everyone on the phone is attractive! You're ringing, and the person responds. Imagine it's someone who advertises a 500 a month apartment. Be kind, say good morning, be honest and upfront and tell him you've just begun a new lettings company, waiting for good tenants (you'll have the moment you start advertising, and I'll be back) and maybe you can let them stay. Sit back and wait for your answer!

Some landlords will under no circumstances speak to agents. Some landlords would not do business with an owner, even if you gave them 10 000 free beer every month. Everything is like that. Life is like that. The landlords are the same as others, some are open-minded and consider reasonable suggestions, others are closed-minded and dumb, some are rude, even abusive. Good luck to them. Good luck to them. All you tried to do was help them let their belongings, and it was their loss if they couldn't see it.

Some homeowners will say, "I just need 500 to cover the mortgage, and I can't afford to pay an agent fee above." That would be great, you should give them that amount of 500 a month, so you leave the property at 550 a month, and that's as close to their price as that doesn't make any difference. Recommend that you through the flat on your 550 books. At this point, the guidance is all you want. The price is secondary in the initial period. Get the directions first, then think about the property later. Say to the landlord, you'd love to put it up for 550, and because it's no lct-no fee, what has the landlord to lose? None, they hire you for FREE, they pay you only if you excel. Most smart people could see the merits of this.

And then the amateur landlords don't know what they do. Maybe they have inherited the home of the girlfriend, and they don't really want to sell it, but they are too busy to chase tenants all day. Maybe they don't know how to find tenants or compare tenants. Not all know this, don't think they're doing it. These landlords are exactly the kind of people you want. They are your perfect customer, and when you meet them, you court them furiously. You will fix them all their property problems and make some money for yourself. Say that they would like to meet you at the property to be allowed.

If you are inclined to do so, make an appointment to see them as soon as possible. Don't make next week's meeting; don't make tomorrow's appointment, what about that afternoon? Within twenty minutes, what about? Enthusiasm is all. Probably in half an hour Huge & Impressive couldn't meet them, but you might. Take your camera and ask if the house is OK to take pictures. Take your notebook and record all that needs to be mentioned. No letting the company does so, don't even think about it, as that would be a waste of time and could lead to headaches if you made a mistake in the future.

Note, you will do anything to land the property, and if it includes raining in ten minutes, do it. You can do exactly the same by ringing small private ads to include in the local paper for land. Ring them up, introduce yourself, and provide your services. If necessary, give them a small discount. Yet note, several times you're going to be backheeled, refused, but so what? You are also invited to do so many more times, I guarantee. Why? Why? Simple, as there are so many new and amateur property owners out there, many of whom are vacant, and many are simply unable to afford revenue. If so, they face the real risk that the house will be repossessed if the mortgage is not paid. Not all landlords roll in cash, it's very easy to enter a buy-to-let home, but it's sometimes hard to get out. The tenants are stuck and just let the house, which is why many are only too happy to hear a cheerful character (You!) who can solve all of your problems. Keep it up, and once you've developed three or four properties, you'll be a step closer to starting your company, really.

It is important that you add real properties to your first ads from the very first day on because that is the main reason why most of your potential customers would read your ad to see what is on hand. Be imaginative, be enthusiastic, be motivated, and optimistic, and you will attract and leave properties. Believe me, there are many desperate tenants out there, and they'll tell you to change their vacant apartments and houses.

Take another look at the advertisements of the other company in the local papers week-in-week. You can pay for these ads only because they produce the company. But here's a word of caution. Each property advertising often receives fewer responses than you have been positive. But this is all right because every property you sell or rent will generate about 1,000 dollars of income, up to 2,000 dollars per year, some more, some less. So you don't have to sign up and let dozens of every ad, but that would be nice. If in a week you can sign up for two or three and let one or two of them startup, then you're doing very well, and your company will grow surprisingly quickly.

When you rent just one property a week, by the end of the year, you would be renting over fifty productive properties. If you do this, you are targetting an annual income of 50,000 dollars (almost 90,000 dollars), and we look at that before all the other revenue sources you can add. Yeah, I know you're going to have expenses, but what does it not do? In my first year, I let twelve properties in a month, and you can imagine how wonderful I was, and you have nothing to impede.

In fact, just the opposite is true, because there are, as I said before, more properties to rent around the world today than ever, and more people seem to want to rent them. Of course, there is competition, but you are on the road to becoming the specialist in rental property in your area because you're learning everything there is to learn and because you are much more knowledgeable than your exhausted opponents who don't really care whether or not you're missing a specific house.

CHAPTER TWO
Choosing the style of investment and right property

Choose the right property

The properties you may find, which one(s) do you buy? In short, the ones that stack up the figures.

For this reason, it is important that you view your investment as a business and not just some form of gambling, although the property market contains a number of risk components, as do most types of investment. Just as you need to know in all types of business that you're going to make money and not lose money, it's the ultimate answer whether you run a profitable business or not. Nevertheless, there are two different categories of high-level ways to profit from property investment, which are discussed here.

Types of Investment

Capital growth–appreciation

This is the most common way for people to think of earning money from property, often because it is the property they own and live in. Such investment is the purchase of property for a single price, and later selling it for a higher price, often known as appreciation. This profit method usually takes time to increase the value of the property. You may, however, add value to the property by doing some work, such as renovation or extension. In other situations, you may be fortunate enough to buy something worthless and sell it for market value on the next day and thereby make a profit from the' right' or the' flip.' You will normally have to pay Capital Gains Tax when you sell the property.

Positive cash flow–income

This is the type of benefit that is typically made by tenants, where possession and distribution of a property are less than their income. This means that if you add up your mortgage payments, management fees, and repair costs, the total should be less than that paid by the tenant during the same period. If you pay £ 500 on overheads per month, for instance, you would like to let out at least £ 550 to make a profit or a positive cash flow. You will usually have to pay income tax on rental profits.

The two types of investment mentioned above are not the only two, and they are not necessarily mutually exclusive so that a property that represents both types of investment can be found. Indeed, most properties will be appreciated in a way, although in recent years, there have been areas with zero growth and indeed areas with negative growth, which means that the value of the property has actually declined.

Similarly, the Positive Cashflow varies, and you can only make your best-informed decision on the day and for the day, in accordance with the market conditions, with all the available information. Historical trends can suggest a potential future, but this is no guarantee.

Plan for Voids

You must add Voids to your overhead or cost structure. Vacancy periods, simply known as Vacancies, are times when you have no apartment but have to continue paying the mortgage and other expenses, such as service charges, for a leasehold home. That is why the most common purchase to let mortgage is based on a 130 percent factor, the lenders expect vacuum and access costs and build a simple guarantee for their financial exposure to you. According to everybody's expectations, 130% is a good rule, so your actual rental income should be 130% of your mortgage payments.

Most creditors and tenants have been robbed because they have to pay their mortgage without the rental income to cover the outgoing cash without paying for Voids and suddenly run out of money. Your land may be vacant for several months in highly competitive areas. It is a good idea to have a mortgage payment of around three months set aside for your purchase. To let in case of avoiding.

The larger properties you have in your rental portfolio, the lower the chance of your mortgage payment payments being cash because you balance the risk of Voids across the portfolio and not just on a single property. Nevertheless, this means that you have sensibly spread your assets across different areas to prevent revenue loss when, for some reason, a particular area is affected. For example, if you have five apartments in one house, all of them will suffer from the same local market conditions. You won't have one, but five Voids to contend with in times of low demand and high competition. If you have five rental properties in different suburbs of the same town or city, your chance of having all five properties empty at the same time has been reduced. Better still to have these five properties in various towns. Don't have all your eggs in one basket, as the old saying goes.

It is important to remember that, whatever the number of properties you have and how widespread they are, they all have a small chance of experiencing Void Periods simultaneously. If that happens, you need a plan, but you can lessen the chance of it by stunning your tenancy periods so that not everyone begins and ends in the same month. Normally this would happen as different tenants come and go at different times.

Yields then Profits

Returns and Profits Many methods are used by people to calculate what they call yield. Yield is essentially the ratio of income generated by the property in relation to the initial input of capital and costs associated with land acquisition and lease. Yields are generally a percentage number, and depending on the area and the person, you will get a different story as to how valuable a yield is. Some people measure the potential income of a property by doing a series of complicated calculations and reach this yield rate, already know their personal limit, and accept 11% yield but refuse a 10% yield.

If you look at the big picture, however, most yield calculations are a waste of time as the conditions on which they calculate change tomorrow. In addition, the idea in business is to make money and do not lose it, so any income is generally a good income, although it is only 5%. Of course, there are practical aspects, but you must remember that these figures can change every day and depend entirely on how you calculate your yield.

The preferred method of determining the viability of a positive investment cash flow is simply to see the profit after your costs. If the flat costs £ 500 a month to run it is negative cash flow of £ 490 per month but a positive cash flow of £ 550. This is all about what you are happy with and how much you need to set up a Void buffer, as mentioned above.

Try not to get stuck with hairline percentage fluctuations where 10% is bad, and 11% are good, rather focus on the real income and what it means for your property business.

The interest-only mortgage is one way of improving your profits in contrast with a regular repayment mortgage. This can significantly lower monthly repayments, but be careful, and you will have to repay full principal loan amounts at the end of the mortgage. This is often a perfect way to pay the main mortgage amount when you expect for 5 or 10 years of a 25-year mortgage. But in the meantime, you have had to pay less each month when you sell it. When capital growth in the property is strong, you can refinance or sell it at the end of the mortgage period and pay the principal back with enough left over to reinvest. It depends very much on what your long-term plans are, but only curiosity can be a useful tool for property investors and landlords.

Different Deal Types

There are potentially an infinite number of ways to arrange a property agreement, there are, in fact, very few rules, and you can be as inventive as you want if you use mortgage financing in order to operate within the constraints of any lending requirements. We could not, however, list and describe all the different options, but we did choose to highlight some of them here in order to show you the kinds of options, the pros, and cons of each of them.

Any money down

This is the most frequently requested kind of offer by real estate investors who are new to the market or want as little cash as possible to invest. When you think carefully about this option, it will soon become a very inappropriate method for investment in property. It looks like you'll get something for nothing, as we all know this is very rare in life, particularly in the company.

For example, the name of this type of deal is a bit of a misnomer because it means that you can own property without putting money into the transaction so that everybody can get the property for nothing if that is real. Usually, some kind of deposit will be paid to protect your interest in your chosen parcel. There will inevitably be copying fees and probably additional costs. But if you succeed in getting the right to buy a lot without having to split a penny, it may have changed the value considerably if your property is built and ready to be completed. It can be good, but often the opposite is true.

If new developments (valued before they are constructed) are pre-valued, the developer often has no purpose more than to sell the bulk of the property to buyers and seeks to extract a high value to make their supposed discounts seem very appealing. However, when the assets are sold, your investment will unexpectedly turn into a nightmare. This is because, as explained above, the standard buy-to-let mortgage relies on the ratio of 130 percent, which can lead to a much smaller mortgage offering than you had expected. The consequence is that you are contracted to buy something for which you have no income. At this time you have only a few choices:

Option 1: Try to find deposit money and any additional funds necessary to make the purchase, this frequently means getting a loan from somewhere or lending money to cover the purchase and you will then have to make mortgage payments on something which will not be issued. This can lead to a downward financial spiral.

Option 2: Understand that the deposit must be paid, but you can not afford to fill the balance and lose the property and your deposit.

Option 3: Try finding someone from your contract to buy you. Although your contract can be transferred to sharks when someone knows that you are back to the wall, they will tie you to the absolute minimum, and you may still be poorer a few pounds away from the deal.

Option 4: You may be lucky to find the future buyer who will return to the deal given the short period to complete, but this is unlikely and quite rare.

Back-to-back

This type of deal has a number of variations, but the basic concept is to arrange the purchase of a property and to sell the same property afterward to complete the inbound and outbound sales on the same day. The idea is to make a profit from low and high sales.

While back-to-back sales on new buildings are made easier, allowing a good lead time to locate a buyer, in many cases, existing properties can be bought and sold as well. It's good fortune sometimes and good management sometimes. If you can trade early and have a long time to complete, you can spend some time finding a purchaser, but obviously, you have to have something in demand and bought cheap.

Cash Back

This type of deal is quite easy, but still has some inherent dangers. The basic concept is to find a property with a market value greater than the buying price and to receive a mortgage on a market value basis. Of example, if you value the property to £ 100,000 and you can buy it for £ 75,000, your Buy To Let Mortgage 85 percent will lead to an £ 85,000 loan that will give you £ 10,000 cashback on purchase. Many applicants are not interested in this type of transaction because they feel that the Lender is dishonest; make sure your application does this before you start. You should remember that your attorney is responsible to the Lender to ensure that there is no mortgage fraud.

Most lenders will only lease on the purchase price, called an LTP, so you have to find a loan that loans the value, which is called a Loan To Value (LTV). The other method is to find a lender that first lends you more than the value or price of the property. Many lenders bid up to 125 percent of the property value from time to time. Often they release the funds as part of the basic mortgage until completed, and other times they release funds for payment of works or improvements. In the case of improvements, invoices or receipts are generally desired and can be paid directly by the supplier of the goods and services concerned.

The only note that your property financing is what is called "highly focused" on this type of mortgage. This means that you are squeezed out of the property as much as possible. The problem is that it typically means that your mortgage payments are higher so that you may have difficulty producing Positive Cashflow from that house. It may also mean that any capital growth in the property takes a lot more time.

Profiting From Buy to Let - Finding the Right Property

In order to take advantage of the rental property, it is most important to buy the RIGHT property at the right price.

Whether local rental demand is strong and good quality renters available overall, it will do little if your investment property is poorly located or unattractive and/or of the wrong kind for the local market. So, it will be a good time to surf the net, build relationships with good local agents, and actually view the properties yourself!

Concentrating on yield

For years, real estate investors have been focusing on potential capital growth and prepared to take fairly impressive net returns of 3% to 4%. This will obviously stop in a property market where there is little inflation, and investors must look at what kind of returns a property could achieve and still regard the property as a long-term investment in capital.

The problem is that in order to capitalize on this developing situation, you need quite serious amounts of capital. Mortgages will still be available, but only to individuals considered to be a reasonably risk of good credit. The days of 90% and 100% mortgages are usually over for the foreseeable future, and this is not bad in the end.

When the boom started in the gold rush days of the late 1990s, it was relatively easy to take advantage of buying to allow. Landlords with the right properties could generate a return of up to 15 percent along with phenomenal capital growth and even a "so" property.

That's not the case anymore. With the tremendous rise in property prices and that rivalry amongst landlords for tenants, it's hard to get a 5.5% net return, so it's very important to buy the' right' property more than ever.

I assume that buying an investment property does and don'ts are not really tough and fast' rules,' and there are always exceptions, but you should follow these guidelines where practical in order to take advantage of your properties.

1. Don't get too personal.

Don't buy an investment real estate just because you want to live in it personally. Always look at it from the point of view of potential tenants.

Furthermore, try not to spend too much on renovating the property. You may fall in love with a beautiful £ 20,000.00 kitchen and a £ 10,000.00 bathroom with taps each cost over £ 200.00, but unless it's a very up-to-date apartment, you'll waste money, because there is a tiling rent for a specific flat or house in a certain location in a certain size.

2. Look for the demand. Who're the guests going to be?

Where are the potential tenants, and who are they? Are there local companies and organizations, such as schools, universities, and even TV studios, which are often employed in short-term contracts?

Flats and houses conveniently located for such places will typically be easy to use.

3. Do be well connected

The old saying,' Place, Location, Location,' is important when it comes to an acceptable Buy-to-Let house. In a city like London, it is always important that the property is a 15-minute walk from a station or at least close to other road connections such as motorways, bus routes, etc. Look for convenient shopping, bars, and restaurants, because these are always attractive for the residents.

4. Don't fool yourself!

When you purchase a rental home, please remember to take ALL costs into account.

Check the Service Charge Check the Ground Rental Insurance (usually included in the Service Charges) Note that during a change of tenants, you may have periods of the void, perhaps up to two months each 12 months, etc.

Note maintenance and renewals Gas and likely energy security controls will cost you up to £ 150.00 a year, but you can probably spend less if you are shopping around.

5. Be careful with things you can't control

If you buy a flat, pay special attention to the ordinary pieces, it doesn't matter to end up your own' palace' in a' slum!' This can often be a problem in a converted property, where the maintenance or cleaning of common elements, such as hallways, drives, and gardens, can sometimes be without formal or, at best, an undefined responsibility.

Finding the property' right'

So what is the property' right?' While it might be blindingly obvious, you pay the right price first of all! Successful buying is all about return on investment, be it the appreciation of capital over the long run or rental return. Nobody will pay you more rental to compensate you if you pay too much.

You should not always choose the cheapest land. Once I saw in Manchester for about £ 12000,00 a two-bedroom terraced apartment. I told anyone who knows this city very well, and she asked me the street name. She said the house was overpriced when I told her!

It's generally better to look for good, buy-to-let properties in urban and suburban areas than in rural areas simply because there are probably far more people in urban and suburban areas seeking lodging. The countryside and the shires are more attractive for nesting, the elderly who settle down or retire–these people usually buy rather than buy.

For instance, someone I know used to rent two bedrooms in a semi-rural location worth £ 270,000.00 and paid for renting about £ 800.00 per month. Most buildings in central London at that time that cost less than this returned over £ 1200.00 a month for rent.

What about Ex-Local Property Authority?

Ex-local property purchased initially under the buying system may be a good investment, but you have to carry out your homework and many legacies. Some council properties were run-down, managed poorly, and have major antisocial behavior problems, but most are all right and do not have more problems than other private city centers.

See the house, walk around the property a little. Are there plenty of graffiti? Is the site generally free of litter? How does it feel? How does it feel? What are the lifts like if it is a high-rise block?

Generally speaking, it is better to be a little versatile. Provide the property with furnishings or furnishings and be prepared to accommodate a guest you think is worth it.

New or Old Construction?

Pay attention when shopping for brand new. Bright, shiny downtown apartments with designer kitchens and bathrooms are so seductive, but not always a good value for money. Very often, the developer has set a price, which is not a true price on the market.

Property Clubs

City Center developments are also favorites of' Property Clubs,' which want to negotiate bulk agreements with developers and to give their members a so-called discount. There are definitely occasionally bargains to be made by shopping in this way, but I personally will avoid them like the plague!

If you have to buy new ones, sometimes it is best to buy the last flat on the block because the developer wants to move on to the next project.

Where is the best place to check for property for investment?

As I said earlier, it is usually preferable to buy the best leases and lowest void periods in urban areas, towns, places with colleges, schools, good jobs, etc. But you should find a property in another part of the UK. It is certainly true that some towns and regions in the United Kingdom are better to rent a property than others.

For a number of historical, cultural, and job security reasons, many northern and midland cities, apart from London, offer excellent leasing opportunities with extremely healthy rent.

Local could be the best

if you already live in or close to a good investment area. I think it is best to first look at your area because you know it best. You can also easily return many times to see if you make the right decision, although that is often very hard when you are faced with a long journey to go back and forth to make the necessary inspections. Once again, local investment was the approach adopted by Judith and Fergus Wilson as they built their purchase to empire in Ashford in Kent.

Is the auction worth buying?

Most people tend to buy property traditionally. They see an appropriate property placed on an offer subject to the contract (in England & Wales), and once accepted, they arrange a mortgage and employ an advocate, surveyors, etc. to carry out transportation and surveying activities. This process can take up to three months, and the purchase of leasing property is a special process.

However, there is a faster way. Purchase at auction. Sell at auction. You may usually buy property for less than historically at an auction, but there are some very significant drawbacks to note. Your offer is NOT' subject to contract,' you will pay a 10 percent deposit plus any auctioneer fees and complete your order within 28 days.

Auctions are, therefore, primarily for people with money, and you are strongly advised to go through the legal kit and to carry out a survey before you make a bid–so you really need to know what you are doing. During times of high real estate demand, sales are usually best left to professionals and owners, as the funds are available, and they know very well how much the property needs to be renovated. And in the case of architects, renovations are, of course, an internal expense.

Please bear in mind that even Scotland's property regulation is quite different from England's. Buying an investment property in Scotland Under England and Wales, an offer from the seller is always "under contract," meaning that either party may at any time withdraw without any penalty right up to the exchange of contracts. In Scotland, people are usually asked to make sealed deals based on' offers over' a certain amount. Confusingly, such deals can sometimes hit up to 20% of the' asking price.'

Once the seller accepts your bid formally, you are locked in a contract, and both parties risk substantial withdrawal penalties. It is, therefore, important to make necessary legal searches and surveys before making an offer.

Although the English system has the issue of electricity and water and people leave, I do feel that the Scottish system is somewhat too static and' clunky.' Personally, I assume that every party placing a £ 1000.00 non-refundable deposit with a stakeholder will easily improve the system by accepting a purchaser's bid formally.

Don't be a' chair investor.' Over the last few years, many people have thought that everything they need to do to invest in property is visited a few websites, enter a property club, and let the club choose the properties they want to choose from.

If you're buying to let or want to build productive property investments, then there is no option to' dirty your hands.' You actually have to view the property yourself-no one will take your money so careful. It can be pretty tough and boring, but sadly, as in slimming, the only thing that works is to eat less and exercise more... no simple solution is possible.

Yield or growth in the capital?

When buying an investment property, it is very important to decide what is more important to you, YIELD or CAPITAL GROWTH, or to combine both?

The way to calculate yield is to pay annual gross rentals, deduct ALL expenses (service charges, land loan, building insurance, maintenance, and improvements) and break into the TOTAL price and add 100 percent to the gross yield. You must deduct any fee from the lettering agent in order to determine the all-important net return.

Don't simply add all of the expenses, including mortgage repayments, delete them from their rentals and say,' that's how much I do.' Such a measure is obviously important, but only for your personal circumstances. In other words, you can afford to pay the mortgage, services, etc. for null periods, but you won't know the real potential for investment.

Despite major disasters, I would say that a good UK property is often a great long-term and potentially medium-term investment. But if you don't care about capital growth, or believe that in the short term nobody will exist, and you need to know if you should buy it to let or simply put it all into the bank, the US will say' Just do the math.' Build the net income and see how it corresponds to current savings rates.

You can't have everything. Generally speaking, when it comes to buying assets, yields, or capital growth. There is generally a trade-off between yield, and capital production-you can get a great return on it, but you typically have to compromise capital growth. Very up-to-date properties often do not yield such a high return but return good capital growth.

Personally, if you are desperately or very wealthy in need of rent as income, I agree that it is better to match well –average yield with average capital growth.

Better benefit As long as you buy in a big city like London, you usually get a much better lease rate from a council property, but you won't get the same amount of capital value. But of course, you will have correspondingly less capital depreciation in the unlikely event that the market falls (shock horror!)! The purchase of good ex-local government property is actually a less risky option in this respect than the purchase of a more upmarket one.

How to Turn Your House Into a Vacation Rental

Turning your house into a holiday rental can at first seem daunting... But it doesn't really have to be. This is a phase you can really trust and appreciate! I set up holiday houses dozens and dozens of times, both for my client and my own homes. I understand all aspects, from ensuring compliance with government agencies' rules and regulations to ensuring that the property has everything essential that most guests need. In ensuring the continued success of my customers in their holiday homes, I often take up the role of "vacation rental consultant," primarily in government agencies and code compliance, quality assurance, and ongoing property maintenance needed to meet current standards in the industry.

So it is important to start with the basics if you decide to offer travelers your house as a holiday home. In this chapter, I will provide you with the five main steps to ensure the success of your holiday rental. As you go through this, I suggest that you consider the fact that your house is in one city or town, that this chapter is a general guide and that your local community feelings, as well as the rules and regulations on short-term rentals, are important for you. Remember that your house is private property, not a hotel, and it must be carefully and carefully prepared and managed as a tourist holiday accommodation.

The very first thing you must do is inform yourself about your local city, country, and state laws, regulations, and rules that make it possible for your house to be a vacation rental in your unique community.

1-LAWS, ORDINANCES, RULES, and REGULATIONS.

Please don't just assume that you can do whatever you want with your property. And please don't spend much on setting up your house as a tourist rental until you rule out the option of laws that prevent you from doing so. Many local and state authorities have clear regulations to establish your house as a holiday rental and that it is likely to have some level of city, county and/or state licensing. Many government agencies also require that you collect local and state taxes from tourists who rent your property to rent your home for a short term rental legally.

A quick search of the news of the rental holiday shows that with short-term rentals becoming increasingly popular, many communities have to license restrictions and very clear rules and regulations for short-term rentals. Call your local city or municipal government offices and reach the appropriate license department to answer your questions. Find out which licenses and/or tax numbers are required to rent and get your house legally. I strongly recommend that you seek the help of an established local licensed rental agency that can help you properly understand and fulfill licensing and tax requirements in your neighborhood.

2-YOUR NEIGHBORHOOD YOUR NEIGHBORS

Now that you have decided that your rent is legal and you have obtained the correct licenses and taxes, it is time to consider the area where your rental property is located. This may seem stupid, and many people gloss over this important step, but believe me that by dealing proactively with this issue, you can save large headaches and struggles with neighbors. Nearly every news item that you read about neighborhoods that oppose or try to restrict holiday rentals points to the same neighboring problems: bright tourists throwing a loud party, local residents parking for tourists, and their garbage are carefree.

I've seen a variety of neighbors to neighbor squabbles over the years in the vacation rental industry, with code enforcement, the police, and even costly litigation. Most of these problems could have been avoided with plain reason and consideration. Find out who your neighbors are and do your best to communicate with them and determine whether they can resist your tourists renting your house.

Once you rent your house to holidaymakers, you must make a commitment to select who to rent your house. It is important to speak to them and determine whether they will fit your neighborhood well. Ask them directly about what they plan to do when they rent your house on holiday. For example, if you find a potential guest who wants to rent your house in order to host a wedding party or a birthday party, consider the impact on your neighbors and whether they're all right. Some properties I manage are situated in neighborhoods that will only tolerate very quiet couples; some of them are designed to accept larger groups, and the neighbors understand the rules. Know your neighborhood and set up your own' House rules' to be complied with by your tourist tenants.

The main complaint about the majority of residents who live next to holiday homes is noise. Some neighbors are more' noise-sensitive' than others, and you need to know if your neighbor will call the police each time a group of holidaymakers sits around the pool and listens to the music. Give your telephone number to neighbors who live by your rent and ask them to call you directly if there is a noise problem. And when a problem exists, call the guests and ask them to relax. Since you rent your house to tourists, it is your responsibility to ensure that your guests are aware of the local district.

3-FURNESS YOUR HOUSE AS VACATION RENTAL

If you've never done it before, your house can be awkward. Below is a very detailed list of basic house furnishings to supply. It includes ideas for bed setups, basic kitchens, applications, and household items. Your visitors should try the simple comforts that most of us find in our everyday lives.

Enjoy building your house for tourists and strive to balance the economy and beauty. When you aim to draw a higher-end clientele, you would like to add a few nice touches and stuff if you were a guest at your own home. You don't have to buy all the new items, but just don't use junk or your house looks like unattractive selling garages. Add some interesting work of art, wall mirrors, artificial plants, and nice nicknacks-just don't overdo them, or they can start to look unwelcome. Some personal pictures (a photo of family or friends) are nice to put on shelves... This reminds visitors of being in some house and not in a hotel.

Suggested Bed Size Layout

Your property needs to be practical, user-friendly, and beautiful to look at. I found the following general layout to satisfy most guests ' requirements. Generally speaking, you will not send the' more the merrier ' message to avoid putting too many extra beds into a single bedroom. If your property has an office or den, it is a nice feature to add a desk or set up a bathroom.

Try to make the master bedroom the nicest. In the nicest dormitory, you would typically have a view, such as an ensuite bathroom, a private balcony, French doors leading to the swimming pool, or patio. Or, if the property has no other value, it may just be the largest space. If you have more than one bedroom with an en suite bath and/or view than if you are fortunate enough to have a property that can be marketed with more than one master bedroom or suite... And that's a wonderful thing. In this way, couples who travel together don't have to flip to the best bedroom!

About bed sizes: after almost two decades in this business, the layout below is suggested and listens to what guests need. It now looks like most people are sleeping in king-size beds at home, and many couples who stay in rentals are insisting on their king-size bed. For certain couples, not getting a King bed option can be a' deal-breaker' as they feel they can not sleep with their partner in a smaller bed. That said, here are the basic guidelines proposed...

Two Bedroom House

Bedroom 1: Master bedroom-Prefer bed king. Use a queen if the room is too small.

Bedroom 2:-2nd Chamber-Queen or 2 Twins. (Two twins are a better choice because they can be pushed to make a king together.)

Three Bedroom House

Bedroom 1: Master bedroom-Prefer a king bed. Use a queen if the space is too small.

Bedroom 2: 2nd bedroom— king or queen or two twins.

Bedroom 3: 3rd bedroom-2 twins or trundle bed Four Bedrooms Chamber 1: Master bedroom-King size bed preferred, but if space is too small, use a queen.

Space 2: Queen or King Room 3: Queen or King space or 2 Doubles. Bedroom 2: Queen or King.

Bedroom 4: 4th bedroom— 2 twin or trundle beds Cookware and kitchen items Equip your holiday kitchen with all basic cookware and kitchen items. Purchase a decent set of good Cookware as much as you can afford. It doesn't pay for the cheapest in the' long run,' as it doesn't last, but doesn't have to buy the best. Sometimes a good stainless steel package can be found in a box. Don't get the cheap things of aluminum.

Stove Top Pans: Include a 2, 4, 8, and 10-quarter basic package.

Skillets: 7 and 10 inch Oven Pans: baked glass dishes: 9X13 & 8X8, lid roasting pot, cookie sheet, silkscreen, one pie pan, two cake pans, one pizza pan.

Bowls: 2 big bowls: 8 to 10 quarters; 2 medium bowls: 2 to 4 quarters; 2 small: 1 to 2 quarts. We may be solid or glass. They can also be used as bowls.

Knives: paring, large potatoes, butcher, cooking, sharpening.

Cook preparation items: colander, spatulas (1 medium size, 1 1 broad size), spoon mixer (1 large, one medium), wire whisk, waist whisk (the best is good manual), plastic cutting boards (1 large and one small), rolling spoons, ladle, funnel, and tongs.

Toaster, coffee pot, blender (good quality to spin the frozen beverage) Other items in kitchen: 2-4 potholders, trivets, table-top places, six dish towels, teapot (for steeping tea; not essential but nice) Breadbasket, an aluminum film, and plastic wrap.

BBQ Grill: The best gas grill is inexpensive — plan to replace them every few years.

Flatware and Service: dining tables, soup, and cereal dishes, little plates (Service for 8 to 10 sleeps), glasses (Service 8-10 sleeping), flatware (Service for ten sleeves), 6 to 8 Serving spoons, two slotted spoons, coffee bowl, cups of coffee or sauces (Service for ten sleeveless), 2 to 3 serving bowls and platters, or perhaps turkey or roast. Bright, colorful serving bowls are lovely and allow the kitchen to add a' color bath.'

Cleaning supplies (guests ' property): Hand dish soap, dishwasher, degreaser, window cleaner, cleaning cloths, 2-3gallon bucket plastic wide, mop, two brooms (1 inside and one outside), one soft-goods pot Guideline Equip your house for holiday rentals with good quality bedding, towels, and window pan. Don't purchase the cheapest soft products. You will not last, and you will probably receive complaints. Guests expect good towels and linens and write poor reviews of poor goods. Through purchasing from a discount shop or home furnishings, you can save money.

Towels: For rental of two bedrooms-towels of 12 bath, hand towels, and eight clothes of washing; for rent of 3 bedrooms–14 towels, 14 towels of hand, 14 clothes of washing machine; for rental of four bedrooms–16 towels for bath, 16 hand towels, 16 towels for washing sheets and pillowcase: 2 sets for each bed. Receive a minimum of 400 sheets bedding guards: mattress covers for each mattress zip pillow guard for each bed pillow (go on the pillow before pillow).

Bedding spreads or comforts: from high-end hotel rooms, we take our cue. In this letter (2011), travelers want couches on the contemporary market (over comforters) and/or mattalesse covers. Bed covers MUST be cleanable.

Decorative and convenience items: throwing pills, 2 or 3 throws blankets, throwing rugs, doormats Beach / Pool Towels–2 per bedroom window coverings–nice curtains and/or blinds An entertainment and Internet Services: flat-screen TV: people expect the TV's in their bedrooms as well as the principal living / big room. I recommend a big TV (min. 36 inches) in the living room and smaller TVs (15-24 inches) in the bedrooms. For security reasons, a small flat-screen TV needs to be mounted on a wall or office.

Cable or satellite television: Do not offer' pay per view ' characteristics. It is too difficult to monitor these charges.

Internet (DSL): WiFi is a function anticipated. Nearly all visitors ride on laptops... And if they don't have internet access, they get angry. Most renters ask for WiFi.

C / D and Stereo players: Some guests fly on today's market with iPods, but most still expect some sort of music player. It shouldn't be a costly unit. It can be a large boom type with detachable speakers and should be large enough not to be taken out by people.

4–Maintenance and housekeeping The holiday must be kept well preserved and tidy. Note that, although your house is not a hotel, you sell it to travelers for holidays, and visitors expect cleanliness and maintenance requirements from nice hotels. This is not a place to cut corners, and if you do, your house will soon appear on the Trip Advisor, Flip Key, and other rental pages with negative comments. Malicious reviews about poor cleaning and maintenance can quickly stigmatize your house and prevent future guests from renting it, even when they are overwhelmed by scrupulous guests. You just have to pay the cost to keep your house to the standard of quality.

Most holiday rental agencies collect the cleaning fee from guests in advance to clean it when they leave. Guests expect and deserve to enter a safe and clean house. Set a cleaning rate that covers your house cleaning costs every time visitors leave. Make sure you plan to keep the house clean and hire a good housekeeper better yet. Ensure that tapestries and furniture are cleaned when necessary. When your house is not rented, make sure that you give it a deep cleaning. Replace new towels and linens as required and never make a bed or make a bathroom with tired or dirty towels or linens.

If your house has porches or decks and outside furniture, you must keep them scrubbed and mildew-free. Every guest who checks in must look fresh. Even with yards, windows, swimming pools, landscaping, and whirlpool tubs–they must be kept to quality standards, or complaints will be received.

This also extends to household maintenance issues. You will improve your skills to make sure that all light bulbs work, that a / c filters are adjusted, that the web works, TV is remote, that toilets are flushed properly, and that the pool and whirlpool heaters work well. You must also be' on-call' to the property and make minor repairs. If you don't live in the same city as your rental, and are fully committed to keeping it, employ specialists to do so. If you are unable or unable to do this or can respond promptly to any maintenance needs, I strongly recommend that you hire a professional rental agency to provide such services. This saves you a lot of headaches and could save your house's credibility.

5-Property management-advertising, bookings, rentals, and bookkeeping The last basic step in transforming your house into a good holiday home is to start an advertisement and make reservations. Today websites with large repositories of rental properties can be picked from several mega holiday rental advertisement pages. Most are designed to allow you to post your own copy of an ad and download your own images. Wait to pay more than $500. get put on-line to find your property for prospective renters. You can also use social media like Facebook and Twitter to promote your property's availability.

You need to be fully committed to every part of the administrative process if you want to manage your property yourself. This includes reacting promptly to e-mail and call inquiries, maintaining a availability calendar, discussing with potential guests whether they are suitable home tenants, writing and submitting guest rental contracts, collecting rental costs, collecting and charging the necessary bed/sales and/or selling tax, collecting and reimbursing deposits (or assessing costs, where applicable). Many home-based reservation management software packages are available to support the organization's life, but they will function only if you keep the information up to date.

CHAPTER THREE
Factors to consider before investing

Mistake #1:

Jump in without the information you need. Fortunately, you are on the road ahead of most people here because you are reading this book! It's just the beginning, but such information can literally save you millions of dollars in the next few years of your life. This is important information. Knowledge.

We live in the' Information Age,' but it still appalls me that the average investor spending hundreds of thousands, if not millions of dollars on the house, is deficient in information.

Going half-cocked away and assuming you know all you need to know is always a disaster recipe.

Remember, now I have been doing this for more than 26 years, so I saw them come, and I saw them go.

However, information products such as this are absolutely invaluable. However, as I said, it's only a beginning. All successful property investors are commonly asked to provide expert advice early and to pay for it. The modest fee for good tips is always far less than the price you pay if you make a mistake with somebody else's money in the hundreds of thousands of dollars.

There's no man (or woman) on an island. Arnold Palmer, aged 70, still employs a coach to help him swing his golf, still at the top of the game after all these decades. There is a' hard knocks ' school and the' prior learning' school. The trial and error methods, which were previously our only options, are no longer required.

Mistake #2:

Falling into love with property The best thing is that we decided to make an offer when we reach the front door. There'd have to be an old cemetery in the backyard to deter us. The gardens are lovely, the house's clean, fresh and inviting, it has some really good bells and whistles, there's something that's indefinable about it, you can't put your finger on it, but it's just the same.

Though you are looking for an investment property, you can easily imagine a great life there. Even though it is a fair ride to the closest schools and the local store is a bit overpriced, which may not last in business for another year, although these fantastic gardens are going to need plenty of water, at least every weekend.

But the downsides have been drowned by the few elements you love-the sunken lounge, the bar, and the new dishwasher. Do not make any mistakes-these things will certainly bring you higher rents and raise house values, but you need to ensure that other negative factors do not overshadow them.

Psychologists tell us that we purchase emotion-then with logic justify. What logic does a convertible automobile have at high speeds of almost 300 km / h? It's feeling, people love them, and they spend more on the budget than they ought to pay. Much later, we will start thinking about the resale value, good production cost, additional safety mechanisms.

The investment in land is no different. Do not in any way influence your feelings about a particular property on your mathematics. Crunch your numbers, see whether these figures work out, weigh factors such as placement and maintenance, get a second opinion from someone qualified, and then go ahead if all goes for you to make money, not lose money. Due diligence is just the world's most boring task-and this is meant to remove the emotion.

Mistake #3:

The Renovation Rule © states: o It will require three times the amount of money and two times the time to get your investment property ready to rent.

You can adequately prepare yourself for any unforeseen expenses using this Renovation Rule ©. And while you are sure to plan for the best, preparing for the worst is always good practice. It's not negative, only if it's.

Let's take an example, then. We can say that you have a nice apartment in the city, beautiful views, great facilities, sweet tapestries, and a tacky old kitchen. You plan on spending five thousand dollars on new carpets and 30 thousand dollars on a new kitchen. You get the keys and start paying the mortgage and take four weeks to get new tenants.

That's your foundation, and for most people, that's the real, inflexible, final plan.

But most people do not know the Renovation Rule©, which changes your budget to permit 15,000 dollars for new carpets and 90,000 dollars for the new kitchen. You will now also allow a period of eight weeks without tenants. Which means you lose money every week. Every week.

A caveat: let me tell you, this doesn't mean that you're going out to spend $105,000 in tapestry and kitchens; this isn't meant to pick you up from the bank to borrow more. The tool is designed to build in safe margins and ultimately to help you purchase the property that you will successfully turn into a rentable property, not something that will lead you to the very edge of (and beyond) your financial resources. Let us say you have a $500,000 budget to buy your property, and you decide that the apartment has $400,000 in value, and you have the carpet and the kitchen made. You would think $100,000 could easily cover that, and most of the time, you'd be right, but what if? With the Renovation Rule ©, it's just on the edge of a no-deal. You may decide to go ahead and take a very small risk, but you will usually be OK.

But what if you can't get less than $475,000 for the apartment? Most people would think' well, we have $25,000 left in our budget, we're going to receive cheap carpets, and we're going to spend the rest in the kitchen. First, it means to accept anything you can get for the money you left. You can be very frightened at the kitchen, where you end up opting for us because of financial constraints and even lower rents.

And the other important factor–what about the period between the payment of the mortgage and the time the new renters begin to pay? Even with the market today, where tenants can stay in no time, your refurbishments take time to complete. You've got to prepare for that. (To this example, I assume that all your costs fall below that figure of $475,000.) If the seller is stubborn, you may have to keep looking. It stops you from...

Mistake 4:

Too much for a property. This is what happens when you make the two previous mistakes-love a property and don't allow enough cash to be saved after a sale. If you are embarrassed to offer a seller a relatively low price, you have to do it if you want the best deals.

Here's the thing: you don't know the situation of the seller. The seller's selling purpose does not influence the purchasing motives unless the museum next door becomes a nightclub. Yeah, they can provide you with excuses to sell, they are heading towards a warmer climate, closer to their families, they want a smaller place, a bigger place, and hopefully, they aren't lying.

But you don't often get the real reasons, and that doesn't really matter. You have nothing to fear, no-fault if you make a' lowball' offer and accept it immediately. It has a lot to do with your "millionaire thinking," as I went through earlier. You might be pleased with your bid, but you insist on putting out feelings of guilt, and you almost feel like you are ripping them off.

Then you have the people who list their property high to' shake the tree.' It's definitely a strategy that you can use when selling, so know it as an investor. Do your homework; offer something less than what you expect them to be OK. If they say no to your first offer, this means they value the property, and you can make an offer again and again.

Mistake #5:

Falling for dodgy investment schemes There are so many people who have been scammed. There are several factors that make it increasingly difficult to pick up the cowboys from honest experts, like the media with a "guilty until proved innocent" attitude.

Now, if you were previously trapped by one of these guys, it's not the end of the world. And this certainly is not your fault, they always seem so professional, and their sales pitch is so attractive, and our government hasn't succeeded as much as we would want, despite their best efforts.

There are also many genuinely honest experts, so how do you differentiate fact from fiction?

1. This is a government website that provides you with information on the latest reports, how they function, and precautions. This addresses tactics that scammers used in the past, such as promising high-risk returns, cold calling telemarketing,' guaranteed rental income,' hard selling to buy' the plan off,' or even flying you to your home, where you will be under pressure to negotiate without independent advice. Browse around this website but warn: the site talks about a number of legitimate business strategies, including free educational courses, motivational speakers that sell books that the government seems to find "overpriced," and they put this in a twist as though everyone in free seminars is a scammer. You're an intelligent, mature adult-without the alarmist attitude of this site you can make your own decisions.

2. Get professional, independent advice-there are several factors to help you decide who you can trust to trust. You can search for business registrations and financial license registrations quickly and easily from there. I see businesses coming from abroad and trying to register their companies in an attempt to look legit, but they are scammers when they provide financial advice and don't have an Australian financial license and try to tell you, they don't need one. All these details can be checked here.

3. There are other 'instant indicators' that tell you that the people with whom you are dealing are real, honest, and true. Testimonials and customer comments are an indicator.

Can they just give you a few people who are going to say nice things? Better yet, can the supplier give you good proof? That means if someone says these comments on the video, the facts are not disputed. Written comments are also good, but if they can't give you two people to do business again, it's a matter of concern. Are they an operation ' fly-by-night'? Were they registered as a business last week for the first time? And were they in the region for many years? Do they promise expertise throughout Australia to tell you that they know every detail about every field, or do they specialize in one area of Australia? They are much more likely to know what you need to know if they are specialized in one area.

The main point is that most businesses and most people are legitimate and competent individuals. The real crooks and cowboys are not as common as you would expect from the media. But they are important there, waiting for the unsuspecting investor for the first time, looking for answers.

Don't let the sales pitch put you off; look for people with no credentials and experience.

Mistake #6:

The under-insurance of your properties goes much further than merely ensuring against fire or natural disasters. There are many landlord insurance providers, and you just can't afford to ignore this area. News and current events seem to always tell of deadbeat tenants who refuse to leave a property, reject rent, even destruction of the complete property without full insurance, suppose who pays the bills? You are unless the damage is hidden.

Insuring rental property is essential for immobilizers and just as important for leaseholders who own valuable goods that would cost thousands to replace. Immobilizers and landlords may be sued for medical payments if someone is injured in or outside their house.

Sudden incidents, such as high-wind windows that shatter, water damaging plumbing problems or theft occurring due to lax safety measures, impact not just the owner, whose property was robbed or lost, who must repair the damaged home. Proprietor insurance does not cover the personal property of a leaser.

Landlords Require insurance to handle various risk insurance policies Landlords vary widely, ranging from simple "name hazard" policies to complete or all-risk insurance policies. Where coverage is limited to certain risks or included in the policy, landlord insurance shall apply to storm damage to the building and to any device and equipment within the unit. The premiums depend on several factors, from the construction of the building to the tenants, and optional coverage increases premiums but offers protection.

Additional coverage may include the elimination of rental damage, property owners ' responsibility for legal defense and medical expenses, burglary compensation or vandalism, earthquake coverage, flood insurance coverage, and cost replacement insurance coverage that pays far more than a regular current depreciation value policy. Landlords can cut their premiums by accepting a higher deductible, not allowing livestock or maintaining excellent rentals. An increase in lawsuits against toxic dark molds is a costly option for many insurers to drop mold coverage, which can still be necessary if the leased property is old or in one of several states that are prone to mold.

The owners of rental properties should understand exactly what their policies contain, what they exclude, and how to file a claim. They should also take photographs or videotape their property, store their own indoors, and keep excellent records of tenant communications. Keeping the property clean and secure could prevent negligence proceedings so that property investors should immediately carry out important repairs. Owners should also notify their insurance agent or claims hotline as soon as a covered incident occurs.

There are so many insurance companies and so many options; this is far beyond the reach of this book. I want to warn you mainly about the dangers of not being covered for any event, which could cost you money. It is very likely that your investment property will be the biggest investment you have ever made, so protecting that investment makes sense.

Mistake #7:

Make it all yourself. One big mistake many investors make for their first time is alone. It's tempting to think you know all about it, people talk about investing tips on TV, you talk to your friends about their thoughts, and you have the bank approval.

No male (or female) is an island. One common feature of all effective immobilizers is that they are all seeking expert advice. Is that not a good investment in itself when you're paying $500, $1,000, or more for advice that saves or makes you tens, or even centuries of thousands of dollars?

You are not alone. You are not alone. You don't have to attend the' Hard Knocks School,' wouldn't it be helpful to choose someone's brains, did it?

Never be afraid to ask for assistance.

I used to keep myself with problems. I never want to ask for assistance. This is because I fear that if I ask for help, my ability to deal with personal problems will be poorly represented. I was too proud to ask for help, in other words.

For example, if all of my co-workers know how to swim and I find it hard to learn to swim, I'll be too proud to ask them to share and teach me how to swim well. I'm afraid they're going to laugh at my failure to swim.

It's normal that people have problems that are too big to solve on their own. It is normal for these people to ask for assistance. Speak to the people around you, especially the elderly. You will find that at some point in your life, they asked for help from other people.

Proper Buy To Let Research Is Critical

First-hand research is important, you can not believe everything that is revealed to you, so you have to do your own work, usually called due care. You can not hold anyone else accountable for your actions, so you have to be as confident as you can of the facts and information that you have. In the world of property, you will always find cases where you have to go with your best guess or your intestines, but these circumstances should be in the few, good research and trustworthy information are paramount.

It is important to remember that if someone wants to sell something to you, they are not usually the best source of factual information, especially when they operate on a commission basis. In addition, when you buy a project via a finder or broker, you can try and convince them that the deal is so good that they buy a few pieces by themselves. This is a strong argument in front of it, but it can often only be a selling pattern, in fact. Consider the fact that the Finder will receive a 1%, 2%, or even 3% Finder's Fee on each of the units they sell, multiply how many units they represent on the development and you will see that they often lose the units they buy (if they actually buy them), as long as they can sell the others. In other instances, the Finder may have bought the units at the front and then sells them for a profit margin or a Finder's fee, only raising his ability to lose any units that he can choose to buy himself. Be wary. Be wary.

What type of property are you going to purchase?

The type of property you can buy is quite literally the type of property you need. It doesn't matter what it is until people want it, and it makes a profit. Today, developers and builders build apartment blocks specifically for investor demand, meaning they can't do any research on the area to see if people actually want to buy and live or rent the property, this is an example of supply. The other side of the equation you are looking for, demand. Often it is better to look at existing conventional housing where demand is easier to determine than some brand new building that has no history. After all, in the city center, there are only so many people who can or want to stay. Obviously, once you have found a field of demand, supply properties must be provided, or you can buy nothing, but in areas of high demand, there are ways to produce supply.

Supplies and demand

In the property, there is an old saying that "location, location, and location" are the three most important things in a property. This is valid when comparing apples with apples so that the one at the best location is usually most desirable out of two similar properties. But it's more important to assess "demand, demand and demand" when looking at Buy To Let. If nobody wants it, there's no point in buying an apartment in a beautiful place. Many people in local areas look at factors like shops, facilities, transport, hospitals, and general infrastructure, but if people don't want to live there, that doesn't matter what is in the local area. In contrast, there may be no facilities at all yet, for whatever reason, people still want to live here. If you are in demand, this is the most important factor to begin the analysis of the house; don't get lost or bogged down in an analysis of the crime rate, council tax, or schools (although these factors may be relevant).

Likewise, you can't buy a flat in the vicinity of a university or hospital and expect to leave immediately; many other landlords usually have the same idea. You may, therefore, face tough competition to let your apartment, which means you normally have to lower your rental in order to compete or to add an incentive, both of which directly affect the profitability of your business.

Some cases may well be true demand near a university or hospital, but you should be led by the demand to an area and an estate and not through the presence or future promises of local facilities. In many cases, the seller will include future developments in the area such as a new railway station, shopping center, cinema complex, etc., and it is best to ignore these facts and focus on "day one" value and status.

How are you going to find land for rent?

Once, it's a question of demand, but how do you demand? The "Pin in the Map" is a simple method.

Before addressing this process, we must digress slightly and determine what kind of return you want on your investment. Do you want a positive cash flow immediate income, or are you looking for long-term capital growth appreciation? Both are not necessarily mutually exclusive; a property can be found that reflects these investment options. In general, however, a single property tends to lean either towards positive cash flow in the north or towards the most productive capital growth in the south. It has to be said that this is a huge generalization, but when you start, it is a very good rule of thumb. These types of investments are discussed in more detail below.

The North-South Divide

You have now determined which type of investment you are most interested in. It is easy to map England and draw an East-West (horizontal) line across the country, approximately between Birmingham and Peterborough. This is your divide between North and South. Now take a pin, close your eyes and stick it to the map, either in the North or the South, depending on the kind of investment you are mainly after. Find the closest city to your pin, and this is your starting point.

Now, obtain the Yellow Pages, the Thompson Local Directory, or any document you want and find all the addresses of the Estate Agent and the Letting Agent. It's generally best to visit the area and walk the streets physically, but you can make your initial telephone inquiries. Call the local letting agents to see if tenants are waiting for rental places, i.e., to inquire. If so, ask for the type of places, one bedroom, two bedrooms, etc. Understand how the local market looks, do people usually want a flat or unfurnished, an important parking space and other dislikes or likes. Many factors need to be considered and asked, make friends with the agent, and talk about what is happening in its immediate vicinity. Local knowledge is often the benefit of an informed decision. Make notes always, you will research many different fields more than likely, and it is easy to forget what has been said. You can also compare what every local agent says to ensure they don't talk hot air or try to mislead you.

Once you have decided what is needed in the area, you can call the local estate agents to find out if properties of this sort are available. Each region is obviously different, and you can not always balance rental demand with sales supply, but you can build and produce supply in several ways. For instance, if you require one-bedroom apartments or studios, a 3 or 4 bedroom house can be purchased and converted. The initial capital investment is more than likely to be raised, and more issues can be addressed, such as permission to prepare, but the returns may also be higher. Two one-bedroom apartments for more than one two-bedroom apartment are generally acceptable. Check the numbers and see if it makes sense. It is worth noting that there are unique laws and rules regulating the multiple occupancy houses' (HMO) specifications, which can make it difficult to enforce an HMO. Check for such costs before you agree to purchase a property for this type of business.

If your selected area lacks the right properties and the rental demand is good, you will always be able to approach and offer owners of the kind of properties you want. This is done by lowering the letterbox with a note, business card, or leaflet. You need to know beforehand what kind of price range you and your region embrace, so if you are approached by an owner, you are ready to discuss your numbers and know your limits. Whatever the conversation or negotiations, you always have to give, even if it's very small, that meets your budget and circumstances. You never know the circumstances of the owner/seller, and later you will be able to renegotiate or even accept your offer if they are in a difficult financial situation.

What are the resources to help?

There are so many tools available to support you in your property study, but everyone needs to make an effort, and the knowledge is not only accessible by itself. You should be vigilant in your studies, as after all, you are interested in financial investment. Do not rely on a single tool for accurate information, cross-reference, or validate from another source.

You can use every single thing to find information:

- There are many websites on the Internet for property research, just check the date of the information.
- In general, newspapers will give you a good knowledge of what is happening.
- Estate agency publications listed in their books at present.
- The window of Estate Agent reveals what is being sold and what is sold, go in and inquire how much.
- Let the latest listings sheet of the agent see what you can let and what the rental is.
- Classified publications such as Loot can be a good local information source.
- The Yellow Pages and Local Directories of Thompson can be useful for locals if you need quotes for the construction or other works.

Do seek to personally visit the area you are searching for to know firsthand, read the local papers to see what happens in the local property market. Do not attempt to compare the locale with another part of the country, and each area has its own specific market and market conditions, which could differ from village to village. In terms of supply, demand, price, and movement, there is no such thing as a national property market. Just focus on one area at a time to avoid confusion.

Make sure you always look at true demand, not just supply dressed to look like a demand.

What kind of tenant do you want?

As much as it is wrong to buy your property on the basis of supply instead of demand, it is also generally wrong to base the acquisition of your property on a particular type of tenant you want to attract. Similar to the above ideas on surrounding amenities, it makes no sense to purchase a nice apartment that urban professionals want to do and pay a lot of rent. Whereas in a high demand area for this kind of land, you can't create demand simply by offering what you believe is needed.

As always, your investment should be based on local information and on how local markets currently stand, not tomorrow, next week, or a year later, but today. Demand can fluctuate, you can't change that, but buying what consumers want now is better than what they could want in twelve months.

When you study the local market correctly and provide the properties local people want, it is you who want the tenants who want their apartment and not you who continually advertise and chase agents and tenants to leave your empty apartment.

Where in the country are you going to buy?

The most common assumption, made subconsciously by those newcomers to Buy To Let, and even by some veterans, is that somewhere in the country, a certain kind of property investor's nirvana can buy and let property. There is no place like that. The best place to buy is where genuine demand exists.

The Best place to buy

It is true that some people have found areas that have been consistently demanded year after year for rental and made a good living from letting properties in these areas. The best place to buy But once a place gets known as a "hot place," each man and his dog floods the area and purchases places to leave. What happens is a simple question of basic market economics; the balance changes between demand and supply, and as the tenants suddenly have so many options, the rent starts to fall as the competition between landlords increases.

The True Cost of Owning a Rental Property

You have found a chance to pick up a distressed property. You think this is a perfect opportunity to turn it into a rental unit for someone else to pay for your hypothecary. Let's take a look at the advantages and disadvantages of your investment before going into a very large purchase.

Mortgage: If you don't pay cash, you'll have a mortgage on the property. When you buy it as an investment property, you pay a higher rate of interest on your loan. As this is a second property, the bank believes your default rate is higher, and the rate is higher.

Mortgage part 2: If your property is not rented for even a month, you will pay your regular living expenses in addition to your investment property's mortgage. If your property doesn't rent for six months, are you adequately funded?

Property taxes: Depending on where the property is located, insurance coverage of the property will range from 0,50 to 2% of the property's value. In many cases, you will choose your local insurance company with an umbrella policy. Besides the regular fire, flood, and earthquake insurance (if applicable), you also need accidental death and rental shutdown insurance. You may want to enter an S company or LLC before you purchase your rental unit. It isolates your property from any catastrophic events.

Corporate management fees: Will you hire a management company? This can usually cost between one hundred and several hundred dollars a month.

Legal fee: fees related to leasing and the removal of a tenant who may be in arrears on his rental payments.

Advertising fees: you would possibly have to advertise your property for rent in the newspaper. Additional options include online advertising and the use of rental agency services.

Repairs: Unknown house repairs will place a significant key in your cash flow. Certain reparations, such as broken tubes, broken housing fixtures, lock changes, etc., take place during your possession, besides the regular updates and drawings.

Providers: You may be responsible for paying for heating, gas/electric, depending on your lease agreement.

Travel expenses: Travel expenses can be large if your property is a long way from home. A rental property is usually recommended within 45 minutes to an hour. Although these costs are typically tax-deductible, you do not want to waste all your free time traveling and leaving your house.

Cleaning and maintenance by tenants: if renters move out, you may need a cleaning company to ensure that you have quality on your house. Reparations may also occur because of rowdy or bad renters.

Closing costs: Closing costs will occur when your property is purchased. Closing costs differ between borrowers and lenders.

Opportunity costs: Your down payment: you will have to deal with your down payment "opportunity cost" in addition to all of the above expenses. You have, for example, purchased a property in the amount of $300,000 and put down $60,000 (20 percent to discourage private mortgage insurance). A conservative way to calculate the cost of your opportunity is to link your cost to a 30-year bond. If a bond pays 5%, your annual opportunity cost is $3000 ($60,000x 5%). This should be added to your transportation costs since the return on capital is guaranteed. If you feel that you have other guaranteed opportunities, consider them, and add them to your total annual operating budget.

Revenue and benefits: Of course, your rental revenue will compensate your mortgage and expenses. To measure the rental market, see popular websites like rent.com or craigslist.org. You can look for comparable units and set your rental price correctly. You will also want to drive around the neighborhood streets to get a better view.

Tax benefits: the tax-deductible is the interest paid on your hypothec.

Depreciation: You have the chance to write down the value of the building you bought every year. Every year you can collect depreciation, even if your property adds value. However, there is a warning. Each dollar you claim reduces your property's cost base. This increases your tax liability when you sell. You simply miss taxes. Please ensure that an accountant is consulted on current laws on depreciation.

Assessment: Although it is not possible to forecast if real estate appreciates in the short term, you can historically expect a return of between 3 and 5% per annum. If a building is held for a long time (10 years or more), there is not a negative return for a full 10-year period in a major metro area. This is where stuff gets interesting. On average, you made $3,000 on a $100,000 home. Remember, the paper profit for $3,000 is only based on 20% ($20,000). It reflects a return on investment of 15 percent. This paper benefit may over time compound and generate pleasant returns after the property has been sold.

Losses and expenses: You will be able to deduct any losses that your property creates. You can also write down travel expenses, repairs, and additions to the property.

It's not for everyone to be a landlord. There are people and individuals to deal with. You may have someone who ruins your house. If they do not pay their rent, you may have to evict a tenant. It is imperative to know the tenant/landlord laws in your state if you are to become a landlord. Every state has its own set of laws and regulations.

Having said that, many owners of rental units have made fortunes. Until buying, there are many factors to consider. You have to determine whether you have the temper and time to be a landlord beyond the numbers.

CHAPTER FOUR
What Tenants Look For In A Rental Property

You need to know exactly what residents look for when searching for a rental property to get the best rent and to attract the best possible residents. With this knowledge, you can make a happy investment and happy tenants.

Location is of great importance to prospective tenants well before they even take the type of house or type of apartment for rent into consideration. You can do little about the place if you've already bought your investment property. If you still are looking for an investment property, take into account how close or far local amenities such as schools, businesses, public transport, employment opportunities, sports facilities, hospitals, ocean, water, parks, etc. are to be considered. Whether the property is on a busy road or a quiet street or cul de sac and if the property offers a view, brises, or the appearance of the property. If buying an investment property, careful consideration of these factors is most important.

The cost of the rental will also specify the type of tenants who would rent the house. The market rental must be fair compared to what is available in the surrounding area. For instance, if 10 of the exact same property is available for rent at $400 per week, a tenant will not pay $500 per week for a property. One of the advantages of a successful property management company is that it has done a CRA (Comparative Rental Analysis) and knows exactly what can and is not accomplished.

Most tenants are aware of safety, and they want to know that they will be safe in the property when out there. The occupant is made aware of issues like barriers at the front and the back doors, surveillance cameras at all windows and doors, and even the alarm system. Some tenants prefer properties that are completely closed to the rear and sides and which have a gate for the property return. It gives them peace of mind knowing that their kids can be safe and secure in the backyard of the house.

The property must be well maintained, clean, and tidy to show prospective customers that you are prepared to provide a safe and welcoming property that you, too, can call home. The maintenance of the property should be viewed as an ongoing (not a cost) commitment to being an investor in the land. This allows you to achieve a higher rate of rent per week and attracts great locators who treat your home as their own. If your property contains drip taps, torn flywire or security mesh, needs painting, or has grown-up gardens, quality inhabitants will be much less attractive. You will be surprised how quickly your investment can be recovered when you invest some money in your house.

The temperature characteristics inside and outside are another important factor. In a warmer climate, air conditioning and ceiling fans are necessary, and ventilation is important in a colder atmosphere. Local residents will know whether they look to a flat or a townhouse, and upstairs the bedrooms will be hot in summer and cold in winter. We are looking for things like a separate air conditioner in the master bedroom or at least deck fans. If the main living area in the house has the hot sun all day long in the summer on that side of the house, it'll likely expect an air conditioner. The same goes for outside, a patio and, if this is so big, the tenants can enjoy themselves comfortably under and not so small, they have to sit inside when visiting their friends or relatives. The house should also be properly airing and have ample ventilation to catch the breezes, which can also save tenants energy costs.

The size of the rooms is also an important consideration in a rental property. You need enough space to live comfortably in the house. The bedrooms don't have to be larger than the Buckingham Palace, but they have to accommodate more than a bed. Children's bedrooms must be sufficiently large for a bed, and a wardrobe (if there is no room), as well as a desk area since most young people, have computers or a television in the room. A resident will also need to see their lounge suite, and other furnishings can easily be incorporated into the rooms. The same applies to whether it's a small townhouse with two bedrooms or a large five-bedroom house.

The investment property must also be poorly maintained and easily maintained. Large amounts of your weekends do not want to spend in a house clothing runs, pruning hedges, and caring for award-winning rose bushes. You want to enjoy yourself, so low maintenance gardens are important. If the property has garden beds, make sure the beds are bordered and mulched. It makes molding and whipping of the pond and weeding of the garden bed simpler for the tenants. If you have lovely gardens and lawns throughout the house, you pay a gardener to maintain them. Not all tenants have the same gardening zeal as you could have. If the property has a pool, I would strongly recommend that a pool service be hired to maintain the pool. That may sound costly, but it can save you thousands of people over the long term.

The climate is becoming increasingly important in today's ever-changing world. With energy costs, higher residents are now looking for rental properties that reduce energy and water costs. Increasingly important to tenants are things such as solar or gas hot water systems in addition to electricity. In the case of two very similar houses, low wattage or energy-efficient light globes installed in the property will also make a difference. The important feature today are reservoirs for rainwater, as people can now be paid for water in the house. When a water tank is brought into the house to power the toilets and the washing machine, the tenants save a lot of water use and energy.

In summary, if you have already acquired property, you may not be able to talk about it but should contain a few suggestions that help not only increase the income the property generates, but also attract a great tenant who will look forward to staying for a long time and thus reduce your vacancy rate.

Having the right mindset for rental properties

Your own property management plan is essential for investing in residential rental property.

Your tenant calls at 8:30 at night and says that water leaks very badly. Your tenant calls at 8:30 at night and says the toilets are obstructed. Around 8.30 in the evening, the neighbor calls and says that a window has just broken down. Your tenant calls around at 8:30 in the night and says the roofs leak. Your tenant calls at 8:30 at night and says the heats are not working. Your tenant calls at 8:30 at night and says the doorknob fell off.

How about a canister is removed. No big thing when it rains, make sure that you don't stand under it. Winter comes where the water hits the ground, pools, and then freezes. Winter is coming. Whoops, someone slips, and you're sued. Big problem. Big problem. It pays to have a management plan for a rental property.

How about this wood outside porch, which needs painting. No big deal. No big deal. Next year. Next year. Next year is coming and going, and you've saved 700 bucks. Three years later, you spend 2000 dollars removing wood, because it rots. Big problem. Big problem. It pays to have an investment plan.

You get the idea, whether something breaks or routine maintenance is important–stuff must be repaired and maintained. A good property management plan ensures that multifamily investment is easy and profitable.

For a good rental property management strategy, there are three main factors. The three major factors are who is responsible for managing the maintenance of properties, who will fix things, and when things will be fixed. Having a plan for these three things is important to keep your rentals. These three considerations should be discussed and taken into account in the rental. It ensures that the tenant knows what to expect in advance when repairs or maintenance are required.

Let's start by who will manage your rental property. Seventeen years of rental experience have taught me that knowing someone else will be better than the owner for managing the maintenance of your rental units. The owner, therefore, controls the most cost-effective rental property management plan.

When you tell me, Oh God, what a nightmare running a rental property is, let me say I learned how to make property management simple and profitable.

In fact, if you understand and execute a sound rental management strategy correctly and continue to invest wisely in cash-flowing multifamily residential properties, your hourly payment time is extremely lucrative.

For example, I personally strongly caution against having a residential property management company.

Can you address who will fix broken items or perform the necessary maintenance?

You, the owner, your payroll, and employed manager, who will actually do the physical work to set up and maintain your rental units. Why should this be included in the property management plan?

Okay, any time anything needs to be replaced, what you don't want becomes an expensive, painful headache.

In asking who will fix it beforehand, you remove two potential problems with your rental maintenance plan.

Second, when a problem happens, you have built a list of contacts in advance. Furthermore, being organized like this greatly reduces tension and encourages the management of your rental property.

I assume that you will see how important it is to know in advance who is responsible for and who will actually do the maintenance activities.

Then I'll tell you the third key to a rentable, easy-to-use leasing management plan.

A few more things to consider about the management of the rental property: if you just start and purchase a house with several families and hands-on an individual, you could want to do as much as possible to maintain and fix it.

When you continue to invest in multifamily homes, it will potentially be difficult to manage your income assets physically.

Understand that rental property management and physical activity are two different things.

If you decide to hire a maintenance worker or a maintenance worker, ask local hardware stores for referrals or ask people to go to a home depot or to Lowes. They shouldn't mention people, but I was pleasantly surprised by how many people moonlight or know that someone is fair and honest.

Search for a handyman in a local paper that you can recommend for maintenance. Call a few people who place adds, not large print adds, rather small adds, and tell them what kind of help you want. Listen to them, ask questions, and ask if they can suggest to anyone for whom they worked in the past. When you check out, tell them you'll call them if you need them.

I do not personally recommend that you employ an outside company to manage your rental property.

Another great place to get trustworthy names for repairs and maintenance is via your local REIA group. The more cost-effective and reliable maintenance men are called and numbered, the better. Put in your cell phone your names, numbers, and what they do or keep them in a special book. I'm sure that I'm not the first or last person to put a name and number in a book and then don't know who they're or what they are doing!

Who would you like on the maintenance list of your rental property before you even need them? A few general maneuvers, an exterminator (I have contracts for trimester prevention with exterminators on all of my units), an instrument repairman when you supply appliances, a plumber, a drainage company and someone to shovel or plow your dwellings, unless you want repairs from the gas company when heating your building with gas.

If you've owned several multifamily buildings, you might want to hire someone full time for physical maintenance. Personally, I tend to have a broad network of contacts that I can call for maintenance and repair work.

When you follow the guidelines for rental property management, it is actually a very lucrative job to obtain and make calls to your cash flow units.

I mentioned before that there was another important factor in managing your rentals.

When are things going to be repaired? Put in the rental or additional arrangements for fixing, twenty-four, forty-eight, and seventy-two hours? Bring it in the contract, so the owner knows how the property is held. It may look stupid, but I have found that the tenants know how to manage and retain their rentals as little misunderstandings as they can.

Note, your duty. Your property has a solid leasing plan and informs your residents how you maintain your rental property will improve your property's own investment property.

Everyone knows the time, as they say in the hood.

How To Market Your Rental Homes

When it comes to renting immovable property, it should usually be left to a professional property manager or property management company to advertise a house, screen and pick tenants and manage rental properties. However, there are some of your real estate investors who, like me, are closely involved in all aspects of your property. Like many of you, we have managed our rental property portfolio for several years. The top three challenges faced by us were to adequately market our rental homes, select the right tenants, and manage the relationships between landowners. We will look at each of the three challenges and share some tips and advice in this tri-part three-month series to help you stay safe and effectively manage your rental houses.

Over the years, we have learned to apply a variety of goals or requirements consistently, which have helped us sustain a turnover vacancy rate of fewer than 30 days per property and an average tenure of 3 years. Moreover, our tenants have always looked after our rental homes so well that we had never to withhold a security deposit.

Look for current rates in your market. First stuff first. You must know the rates for rent in your area. One of the biggest errors landlords make is not to investigate thoroughly what their market rates are. Many landlords just ask for the same or slightly higher rent than the last tenant. This approach, especially in the current immobilizing market, does not always reflect the direction the local market has taken. You must, therefore, do your work. Start online and see what others are asking for similar properties as yours. Most of the properties are not announced online, so you want to know your area. When you start your property in the neighborhood, every house you rent should be fully informed about, and what the rental is. Call each house for the rental sign you see and talk to the owner or manager of the property. Ask them what they want to rent and why. Ask why you are freely informed about the local market many times. We contacted a property officer on several occasions to inquire about the rental and found that, for example, his property is on the market for 90 days, and the prospects for the rental tend to be about $1,100. It is essential to have such information to reduce the length of a vacancy. If you do not have similar rental houses in your division, slightly extend your quest. The more work you carry out accurately your perception of the current market rate in your field is.

Place your rent competitively. Once you know that the rent you are asking for is $1100 to $1300, you need to find out what the rent you are asking for will be. Of course, you want to get as much as possible for your property. Nonetheless, you do not want more than required to prolong your vacancy. You should also be able to explain to a potential renter why you ask what you do. If you have researched in advance, you should have no problem answering these questions. Resist the temptation of renting on the basis of your mortgage payment. Your mortgage payment has absolutely no influence on your area's rental market. A more appropriate means of determining rent are by taking an average of what the comparable rental properties are. Therefore, if you have four properties in your subdivision that are exactly or almost exactly the same as your apartment, spread equally between $1,100 and $1,300, a good rent would probably be about $1,200. We say "about" because everybody wants to feel like a compromise has been made. So, you probably want to think a little bit more about what you really want to get. This could be $1,225 or $1,250, in our hypothetical scenario. Your goal here is not to be automatically ruled out because your rental is the most expensive rental in the area. You don't want to give away the cash, too. This average lease rate approach still works very well for me. Start advertising your rental for at least 30 days. When you know what the current rent rates are in the neighborhood or area of your property, it is time to start publication. Ideally, you're looking for your rent locally and start advertising your home rent at least 30 days before your expected vacation, but preferably 60. The best place to start advertising is through ads on household rentals. In our experience, online rental prospects typically check 30 to 60 days from their expected move date. It is important to get a head start from online advertising. As prospective tenants are increasingly looking for a rental house on the Internet and the display on the web is exactly what you need to start with. However, your advertising plan can't stop there.

I have found that a significant number of renters ' inquiries come from rental prospects in search of homes for rent from 30 days before your intended holidays up to 30 days after your holidays. Anyone driving through your property should know that your property is available for rent, and they should know how to contact you immediately. The signs for your land should be accessible and put in your property's highly visible areas. The queries and guidance created by signs on your rental property are as good as online ads. That is why both should be included in your plan.

Open Household on weekends. Hold Open House. Let's face it. Let's face it. Holding an open house is a very effective way to show everybody who is interested in your property at a convenient time window. You can advertise online your open house and avoid making extra trips to your property to present off to someone who is not allowed to appear. Open houses also encourage you to speak to prospective tenants in person and more easily "sell" your rental home features. It is so much more convenient to see your home rental in person than showing photos online. One thing we like about open houses is that they help us "tweak" our local market knowledge by allowing us to talk to a lot of prospective customers in a short time.

This helps us understand what the marketplace of the people really is. After all, if the research shows that a decent rent is $1,200, but every prospect we talk to is looking for something in the range of $1,000 for a couple of weeks, then that gives us a good indication that our rent request is still too high. Open houses can ultimately be very effective. Each Saturday and Sunday, we did open houses for each of our vacancies before we found the right tenant. And only because the yard signed the saw advertising our open house, half of our tenants found our land.

CHAPTER FIVE
Landlords Guidance For Rental Property Gardens and Outside Spaces

Property owners are probably well aware that many areas suffer from over-supply of apartments because the demand for rentals in the speculative development has been surpassed. One reason for this supply potential is because many of the trendy young tenants to whom these apartments were built are actually more cautious than both developers and property investors predicted.

Landlords should reflect on the fact that many tenants, young and old like a garden, as old as that might seem. An external place in which to sit down or even try a little horticulture or more agriculture, as higher food bills make us all a nation of small farmers.

Landlords are aware that the tenants do not need space, even the smallest external area will add another dimension to the property that the landlord hopes to require. The good news for owners is that it can be produced with little effort or effort-for landlords. It doesn't have to take the time or heavy maintenance, either.

I give some tips to landlords of Belvoir Lettings letting agents who have asked some of the letter agents to build an impressive low-care garden on a budget: what are the advantages of having an outdoor investment property for landlords?

"Located outside properties will increase the living space of a residence and become especially popular with youngsters who do much of their fun alfresco or barbecue," says Neil Jones, owner of Belvoir Cambridge. "Family families with small children are also saying they are drawn to properties with space for their children to run around or have a paddling pool. Even tenants with pets outside are a real plus." A well-designed front garden can also make a major difference when a potential resident comes to a property for landlords. Also, gravel drives should be weed-free and in pristine condition.

There can even be a bonus on the monthly rent you can apply for,' adds Neil.

How can I increase the size of a small space?

"Landlords should make a plan, and they should stick to it," Neil says. "Mapp your space on a piece of paper and fill in your details like a puzzle, remembering to keep ideas simple." If landlords have room for a small flower bed, choose a maximum of five different types of plants, and avoid spreading rapidly. It is also very convenient for property owners to have a different color scheme, alternating between two or three colors, such as lilac and yellow or white and pink. When property owners can not find room for a flower bed, clever use of pots and containers can give rise to a space illusion. Cluster them in corner spaces in groups of two or three or line them in front of a border.

The landlords need to build up with large bushes and shrubs such as a bamboo plant. A high trellis is suitable for grapevines like clematis, sweetheart, and morning glories. If property owners have space, a higher deck or steps to a staged sitting area can also appear very dramatic. Landlords should also seek to establish a focal point of the garden with a tall vine, shrub, or tree. And property owners shouldn't forget these sweetly fragrant plants like jasmine, roses, and sweetpeas–their exquisite perfumes make a small room even more enjoyable. Even the smallest room will smell magnificent.

"When tenants have a lawn, borders, or shrubs, make sure they keep the area clean and cut as much as you can," Neil says. "The overgrown shrubs or weeds would make the room smaller and less desirable immediately." How can property owners manage their garden poorly?

"For a whole year, low-maintenance garden owners should replace lawn areas with paving slabs, slabs, or gravel and focus the garden on an attractive seating area," Neil says.

An elevated platform or decking will generate visual interest without ongoing maintenance. Patios and sheets are extremely labor-intensive, but a ready-made decking kit for home installation is a practical solution that can normally be assembled in one day.

"Again, landlords can pick plants which do not grow wild and spread too rapidly, and these can be removed quickly," Neil continues. "Smart planting can create the impression of a healthy garden even during the winter months." And property owners should note that pots and containers are much easier to maintain than floodplains. But watch out for the aged pots of vintage. They might be attractive, but porous pottery can be fragile and not last more than a few seasons. Proprietors should stick to robust lightweight or glazed containers that can withstand extreme weather conditions and should last as long as your property is available.

Who's the job of taking care of the garden? Landlord or landlord?

"Unless otherwise stated in a contract, the general maintenance of the garden is usually the responsibility of the tenant, much like maintaining the interior of a property in good condition," says Neil.

A landlord is still responsible for structural problems, like fence or tree surgery, but daily maintenance is the responsibility of the tenant-this makes a low-maintenance room usually most attractive for potential landlords such as mowing the lawn and weeding gravel.

A landlord may want to give their tenants a lawnmower and other necessary gardening equipment.

How can landlords build a splendid budget garden?

"Everyone is working on the secret of creating a low-budget yet well-stocked garden," says Neil.

"Early planning ensures that you can benefit from the end-of-line sales of cheap furniture, paving, and trellises in garden centers. Even cutting-edge plants can be available at certain times of the year. In addition, if you have more than one house, you can purchase large spreading plants that you can divide between the two gardens."

Tenants also have to invest in good pots that tenants will not have to repair by a split–landlords can sometimes buy these in charitable sales, on markets, or in-car boats for a few pounds.

"However," continues Neil, "landlords can buy seedlings returning to the web year after year for mail-order gardens–their bulbs and seeds often have a better price than the highways and can sometimes be bought in bulk for a reduced price."

Landlords Raising Rents on Rental Property - Advice on the Tenancy Agreements

Letting companies see rising rental demand as buyers and foreign workers postpone their purchase of homes for the first time despite continuing uncertainty about UK house prices.

Letting agents in London and the South East, in particular, are up to 25 percent more involved in their leases compared to a year ago. Much of this demand comes from young professionals and urban workers who are unwilling to play and buy property on a poor home market.

The consequence of this boom in property environments is the rapid increase in rents in certain areas, as potential tenants are vying for high prices. Reports show that tenants are able to secure large rent increases in these' rental hotspots.'

In the Westbourne Grove branch of Winkworth, Lucinda Richardson said tenants who renew their contract typically pay 5-10 percent more annually, while new occupants pay 20 percent more per annum than they would have done a year ago.

Therefore, what should the landlord do if he is lucky enough to own a residential investment property in the areas of high rental demand? First, landlords should always be careful to offer a tenant a long term contract in areas where rental demand is strong, and rent is rising, compared to the standard six months fixed term. Glynn Judd, head of lettings at Kinleigh Folkard & Hayward Surrey Quays, reports that he knew of tenants who were pushing for a fixed-term tenancy of 18 months even two years. This is because the majority of tenancy agreements, once negotiated, do not authorize a landlord to increase the rent in this fixed term.

So the initial rent that the landlord decides will look attractive at the beginning, but will it still look so good in 24 months? During this time, the landlord can legally have raised rent three times by a regular fixed term of 6 months. The other choice for a landlord is to choose a standard tenancy.

Why landlords may increase their rents A fixed lease How a landlord increases the rent depends largely on the form of tenancy. Many property owners use a fixed-term tenancy agreement like the one on Property Hawk. In most cases, a landlord opts for a lease of 6 months but can be longer. It ensures that you, as the landlord, can not rent during this time without a tenancy agreement, unless certain conditions are laid down in the tenancy agreement. For example, these specific provisions can be an escalator clause specifying that the rent raises inflation after six months.

The overwhelming majority of property owners avoid such provisions. This is because they are considered overly prescriptive and uncompromising. Some tenants tend to test the rent before choosing to redeem at the end of their fixed-term tenancy. Therefore, a landlord will evaluate the prevailing market conditions and decide what the rental market would show at this time. For areas such as central London and parts of the south-east, for example, rent inflation is well beyond general inflation, so if a landlord records inflation, their profits will fall behind the economy.

If an occupant wants to replace the current tenant, then it is fairly easy to raise the rent because it all requires creating a new, safe, short tenancy with the new rent included.

Periodic tenancies

Periodic tenancies The other form of the tenancy a landlord could use is. These are tenancies that do not have a specific end date. The two forms of periodic tenancies are the contractual periodic tenancy for which no end date has been set from the beginning of the much more common standard legislative tenancy. The formal daily tenancy happens when a fixed lease lapses.

The rent increase for daily tenancies is somewhat more complex, as the landlord has to go through the structured process provided for in Section 13 of the Housing Act 1988. If the landlord wants to raise the rent and plans to keep the tenancy on a periodic legal tenancy, the landlord can use the special formula entitled "Landlord's Notice," which proposes a new rent under a certain agricultural occupancy or periodic tenancy often referred to as the 13th Notice. This method allows a property owner to demand a raise in rents once the tenancy begins. A landlord could use that same form for contract rent, to suggest an increase that would take effect 1 year after the tenancy begins. In both cases, the rent payments on a weekly or monthly basis require a period of raise notice (more if the rental period is longer). With both existing tenancies, a landlord may request additional rent increases at the first annual intervals.

There're a number of potential snags for landlord when the rent is raised. There are potential snags for landlords. Not least among these, the rent cannot be borne by perfectly good tenants. A landlord must, therefore, be assured that they will be able to afford the new rental to his current tenant or that he can quickly fill any vacancy and prevent a prolonged vacancy.

Secondly, the problem with changes in section 13 is usually only once a year for a landlord. In a fast-moving market such as that which is currently experienced in parts of London and the South-East, annual rent increases do not keep pace with market rents which means that, by the end of the 12 month lease period, a landlord will have a rent below the open market and thus lack potential rental income.

The other aspect of a landlord having a periodical tenancy that is subject to section 13 is that he is entitled to apply to a Rent Assessment Committee for a tenant that is unsatisfied with the rental increase to determine the rent a landlord can reasonably expect to pay if he or she is leaving it to the open market on a new tenancy under the same terms. The committee is entitled to agree to rent or to rent more or less. The rent then set by the committee is the legal maximum to be charged by the owner. This new rent will be payable from the date specified in the Notice of the landlord unless the committee considers that this would lead to an undue difficulty for the tenants, in which case a later date can be specified. The landlord is able to propose an increase of the rent a year after the date of payment of the rent decided by the committee.

Rent Assessment Committee Power All this can sound rather daunting to a landlord. The truth is that it ought not to be. Although the Rent Review Committee claims to have a significant amount of power in front of it, they simply do not. In the beginning, new rent can only be set if it is clearly unfair. The other factors which limit the range of the Rent Assessment Board and the tenant at rental levels ultimately are that the landlord retains the right to issue a notice of section 21.

This means that if the fixed term period ends when the notification ends that the landlord ultimately responds to an unsatisfactory rent, it is to recover possession of the rental property and simply re-let it to another tenant in the rent he and the market will unload.

CONCLUSION

What are landlords supposed to do?

The easy answer is that property owners should typically opt for a fixed tenancy agreement, such as a free tenancy agreement within Property Hawk's Property Manager. A landlord should avoid the lapse of the tenancy and regular tenancy. You can do this by passing the motions to issue a section 21 notice of ownership even at the beginning of your tenancy to ensure that a landlord will terminate the tenancy. Thus, at the end of the term, a landlord is in the perfect position to either return an existing tenant to a higher rent or, if the tenant objects, regain possession and then let another tenant with a higher rent buy-to-let investment property.

A word of caution for landlords in areas of less competition. The tenants can be disturbed by receiving a section 21 notice at times, and therefore, a landlord must approach the sensitivity of the situation and explain that the Notice is simply a formal process and has no intention of seeing it through. The truth is that even if a rental is not the absolute top rate, it is much better for every landlord than not paying rent at all!

HOW TO INVEST IN REAL ESTATE

How to Create Wealth and Passive Income with Real Estate Investments.

Williams W. Scotty

© **Copyright 2020 by Williams W. Scotty**
All rights reserved.

This document is geared towards providing exact and reliable information with regards to the topic and issue covered. The publication is sold with the idea that the publisher is not required to render accounting, officially permitted, or otherwise, qualified services. If advice is necessary, legal or professional, a practiced individual in the profession should be ordered.

- From a Declaration of Principles which was accepted and approved equally by a Committee of the American Bar Association and a Committee of Publishers and Associations.

In no way is it legal to reproduce, duplicate, or transmit any part of this document in either electronic means or in printed format. Recording of this publication is strictly prohibited and any storage of this document is not allowed unless with written permission from the publisher. All rights reserved.

The information provided herein is stated to be truthful and consistent, in that any liability, in terms of inattention or otherwise, by any usage or abuse of any policies, processes, or directions contained within is the solitary and utter responsibility of the recipient reader. Under no circumstances will any legal responsibility or blame be held against the publisher for any reparation, damages, or monetary loss due to the information herein, either directly or indirectly.

Respective authors own all copyrights not held by the publisher.

The information herein is offered for informational purposes solely, and is universal as so. The presentation of the information is without contract or any type of guarantee assurance.

The trademarks that are used are without any consent, and the publication of the trademark is without permission or backing by the trademark owner. All trademarks and brands within this book are for clarifying purposes only and are the owned by the owners themselves, not affiliated with this document.

INTRODUCTION

Do you ever wonder what an investment in real estate is? It glorious and, at a time, daunting to everyone. "Yes!" To make a successful investment, you must first educate yourself, then take action immediately to introduce your fresh skills and later decide which path you'd prefer to take.

There are directions you can take when selecting the right platform for estate investment, such as becoming a rehab investor, rental property investor, or wholesaler, from there you have plenty of sub-group that get a lot into investment strategies deeper.

If people as an investment in an immovable property typically have to do with finding an excellent property below market value that will produce short or long-term profits. Whether it's residual income or wholesale purchase profits and retail sales, it all depends on what the land has been bought for. It will also determine what is known as the return on investment, depending on whether you want to sell or hold as a rental property. Primarily, it depends on how much money you have invested as opposed to how much money you have in return.

In reality, becoming a full-time or part-time investor is easier than you might think, contrary to popular belief. Investing in property, however, is not for the weak of the heart or the week. It needs continuing schooling and, most importantly, skills for citizens. That's Right-People Skills The minute you can find out that it's all about people and not houses that will explode your market. Note, people are having problems, not homes, and they need you first to help them solve their problems. You'll get the house once you can help solve your problem.

The numbers are always looked at first by a smart real estate investor. From the outset, they have to make sense. Remember that if you don't buy it after you make money. Never fall in love with an estate, too. Speak of it as a tool to get the money you're looking for.

This is a widespread mistake to see lots of newbie investors make. We love a house, and the numbers go out the window. This is a potential disaster that almost instantly causes you to fail. Save the part of your dream home falling in love and focus on the numbers.

CHAPTER ONE
How To Invest In Real Estate Are You Investing Correctly?

The real estate market has been recognized for individual and corporate investment vehicles as one of the best sources of passive income. Once an individual has purchased a piece of property, they can sit back and wait for their renters ' monthly rental income. Anyone who knows investment properties knows this isn't as easy as it sounds, and that's why: reading through this book that skims over the steps in how to invest in real estate won't tell you all you need to know. There are tips for getting started in the most accessible and efficient way to spend. But this is not as easy as experts find it. Let's cover one of the reasons why it doesn't seem so easy.

There are specific property styles and places that are best suited to individual investors. The attraction of investing in rental properties is based on the prospect of regular rental income and the property's expectation of value appreciation. These only come true when selecting the right property in the portfolio of an investor by following the correct knowledge that you can't just get anywhere. The best source of knowledge acquisition is from people with more expertise than you do.

Apart from the nature and location of the house, individuals who want to know how to invest in property should also consider how much they have to pay to buy their home. The financing options offered by banks and financial institutions make it much more convenient to purchase rental properties today. Nonetheless, property owners should ensure that their property's debts are protected by the rental income they receive from their tenants. But one of the essential skills to learn by screening them correctly is how to get trustworthy tenants.

Some steps that rental property owners can take effectively address the challenges of being a passive landlord. Among the essential skills you can learn when investing is just looking at a large number of properties, so you don't get emotionally attached to any individual. Getting going today in preparing your investment in real estate rental property should be the last one on your list if you want to experience the increased steady stream of revenue into your bank account. Still, it has to be set up correctly.

Without doing any research, you cannot hope to reach the real estate rental property business. Though, you can be sure to have a comfortable ride with your rental property business with enough time and effort to set up your rental property. If you get a sound investment plan you've learned from an experienced investor, you're going to avoid a considerable number of mistakes you'd have made otherwise. This book has prepared some essential tips on investing in real estate for you to enjoy!

How To Invest in Real Estate Without Using Your Own Money

Over the past five decades, real estate investment has gained popularity. Although this market has numerous opportunities for large profits, property ownership, and the purchase is complicated compared to investing in bonds and stocks. Learning how to invest in real estate for one to increase their wealth is therefore essential. The following sections identify the different forms and consequences of real estate investment.

Fundamental Rental Property This is the oldest investment type. In this scenario, an investor would buy and rent property to tenants. Then the landlord will be responsible for the payment of mortgages, taxes, and expense of rent. Ideally, the fees of the tenants bear these expenses. In other situations, before mortgage repayment, the lender can charge extra to cover costs. Still, it is prudent to exercise patience and only bill for expenses until the mortgage is paid. Some rent is going to turn into income at this time.

In fact, during the mortgage period, the property will have value appreciation. The asset of the landlord will be more valuable in this regard. What may seem like an excellent investment has some downsides? One may end up with tenants who, in the first place, destroy property or, worse, neglect tenants. It leaves you with bad cash flow. The issue of the property is situated correctly. Also to where individuals like to rent, one should choose an area with low vacancy rates. One should remember that there are tremendous obligations in this form of investment.

Real Estate Investment Factions These are similar to joint property rental funds. It provides a good option for those who want to buy rental properties, but don't want the hassles of being tenants. In this scenario, a company will purchase or create a series of condos or apartment blocks and allow investors to buy them through the company to join the party. One investor may own several or one units, but each unit is controlled by the company that runs the investment faction. The business takes a percentage of rent in exchange for care. The performance of the investment group relies entirely on the company that provides it. By principle, investing by real estate is secure, but factions are vulnerable to similar charges that irk the sector of mutual funds. Research plays a vital role, once again, in understanding how to invest in property.

Real Estate Trading These traders represent a different breed from traditional landlords buying and renting. They purchase properties to temporarily hold them, often for 3-4 months after selling the property for profit. This form is also called the features of flipping. This takes place based on buying properties that are either substantially undervalued or reside in sweltering markets.

REITs These are investment trusts that arise when companies use money from investors to operate and purchase income properties. Similar to other stocks, people trade and buy them on the leading exchanges. This investment form does not include corporate income tax, while traditional companies would pay benefit tax during which they would have to distribute profits as a dividend if they choose to do so.

Now that you know some of the basic terms of real estate investment, you're ready to find out how to do it without your own money.

MAKE Investing Successful Since investment in real estate is such a successful money-making enterprise, there are many different ways people think they can do it. If you're looking at how to invest in real estate, joining a real estate club should be your best approach. The explanation that as a beginner, this would be so valuable to you, is that you will never get their experience from anywhere else. You will be able to figure out what type of investment you want to make after you join a club. You will either buy properties to rent or resell at a later date when it comes to real estate.

Once you know what type of investment you want to make, your next step to learn how to invest in real estate is to look at valuation tips for learning. You don't have to get your valuation license or anything, but you should get an idea of the value of the property. This will help you decide whether a property is worth investing in time and money. When you look at a park and think it's worth more than they ask, but it isn't really, you won't be able to make any money. You have to have as much information as you can support yourself.

Experiencing it is another step in how to invest in real estate. The thing about investing is that you're still learning something new. Those who have been investing from time to time for 20 years are always learning something new. That's why, instead of waiting for you to know anything, you should continue because you can't do that. First, beginning with a smaller property is one of the best tips for a new investor. Since you are not yet well versed in finance, you need a point of departure.

You run the risk of losing all your money on the first investment when you make your first investment in a considerable risk house. Before you begin to take huge risks, you must accumulate some cash. If you start to lose money, you'll keep on doing that. You should try to buy your first property with someone from your club if you want to know how to invest in real estate.

TIPS on how to invest in real estate is a big game these days. Hordes of people are investing in their vast amounts of money. Sadly, they're not all making the kind of money they dream of.

Investment in real estate has the potential for immense profits. But the housing market is also valid in the tank. Most countries still have to deal with the real estate bubble bursting.

So, it's only natural for those to want to learn how to invest before bringing their hard-earned money into the real estate business.

You need to learn how to invest in real estate and play the market wisely if you want to make profits from your purchase.

Goals: The investment isn't like running a $10 retail store and selling it for $15. It would help if you were very specific about your priorities before you invest. Do you want to rent the house, so you get an excellent monthly return from the mortgage, or do you want to flip the house and sell it at a decent profit? The property in which you invest must be aligned with your investment objectives.

Funding: Your investment goals should calculate the funding choices. Purists, for example, may advise you not to take an adjustable mortgage as it has led to many problems. But if you want to flip the property and you are sure that before the mortgage resets you can sell it at a profit, then an adjustable mortgage is a fantastic option. You only need to pay interest and pay the principal to the next buyer! If you are looking for a long-term investment, on the other hand, it's better to have a fixed mortgage.

Smart selling: if you want to sell your property for a nice profit, giving your property a facelift makes sense. Keep in mind that the facelift (refurbished bathrooms, better lighting, or a paint coat) that cost you a few thousand dollars, but it will significantly add to your property's value. Hire experts whenever possible only if you are unable to do the job yourself.

Research market trends: the environment of the property is vulnerable to unexpected dramatic changes. The only way to be at the top of the market is to study patterns and be up-to-date with the latest details carefully. Read classifieds, search for more information, and track what's going on in the market.

Expert support: The majority of people who want to invest in real estate may not know how to invest so that they can make profits every time. People often agree that the profits or losses they make are a matter of hitting and missing. Some of their actions have hit paying dirt, while others have struggled. A real estate agent or investment specialist will increase the chances of success. Hiring a paid lawyer is an excellent way to avoid legal troubles and other stumbling blocks. Your advisor has the latest real estate market knowledge, not just in your immediate vicinity, but in far-flung areas. We will, therefore, direct you in your investment venture in real estate.

Note, the property market is a gold mine for someone who knows how to sift the gold dust out of the desert!

How to Invest in Real Estate During Depression Of Economic

If history is value to us, then looking at past depressions and recessions shows that real estate value declines during such periods. This is due to tight credit-credit is scarce during tough economic times, and interest rates are a high-only tiny percentage of people get credit and only economically sound business proposals.

Through economic depression, there are more sound investment areas: precious metals, food, and energy-the essential elements. One might argue that precious metals are not necessary, but people use them as wealth preservation (especially when there is a possibility of hyperinflation on the horizon), so it is required. But if you're inclined to invest in real estate, read on.

Depression can be either inflationary or deflationary. Deflationary in the U.S. in 1930-goods and services prices fell, and liquidity became scarce. In such a scenario, they lose value businesses and prudent individuals who keep money when boom time and are now buying real estate for investment, generation that is coming, or development of business. Residential property prices are falling based on the region-less glamorous or away further from major employment centers-the more fabulous the fall in prices.

The world is currently in a state of crisis-goods, and services prices are falling as a result of weak demand. Current low-interest rates are supposed to encourage new house purchases and leap into the real estate market, but since buyers are stuck in debt from past excesses and are trying to pay it off, very few of them are on the demand of the new house.

Governments in many of the world's developed countries are bankrupt and are unable to repay the massive amounts of debt they have accumulated over the past few years. Just two potential outcomes are possible: recession or significant devaluation of the currency. Depreciation of money is out of the question because all governments are trying to devalue their respective currencies to become more competitive right now. What happens when everyone tries to pull the blanket their way-either it works out, or the coverage is ripped apart.

One of the major countries ' bankruptcy will have a domino effect, leading to the world monetary system's bankruptcy. Over the past 50 years, economic expansion has been powered by credit; and money printing has succeeded in the past bubbles because they were relatively small, but bubbles have grown bigger and bigger every time, and now we have a financial crisis-a mother bubble. Who is going to lend the lenders money? Printing presses-a vicious circle leading to hyperinflation and eventually recession and the emergence of a new monetary system backed by precious metals. Hyperinflationary conditions are also not ideal for investment in real estate-prices lag far behind the inflation rate.

In such bad times, what is real estate investor to do?

Next, what not to do: don't use any credit unless you get a low fixed interest rate for the duration of the loan and no inflationary changes to the principal (dream of getting that!). Okay, you never know the truth to be told, you might consider some desperate willingness to lend on such terms.

Furthermore, investment for value:-If you purchase a residential property, it is easier for the property to have good tenants who have been living in it for a while. Avoid ghost towns-areas where rent or sell more than 20 percent of homes. When the property is not leased, look for rent prices around the city and deduct 25 percent from it-this will be the price for which you can rent realistically. Buying a rundown property has a good value, giving it a nice facelift on a budget and earning more rental income as a result.

When you purchase a leased commercial property, the same rules apply as above. If it's a storefront, it's best to be in a high-traffic area. Do not enter office space with a mile-long post right now. The bubble still has to break!

- If you are looking to buy an income property
- A parking lot, a generating farm, a reforestation project, etc.
- do your DUE diligence
- don't trust sellers to anything
- You never know what the temptation to sell to them!

In a desperate attempt to get rid of a bad business, there are some business owners faking income statements. Go to the bank to review their accounts-if the seller fails to carry out any proper financial tests-run away.

How to Invest in Real Estate Outside The Area With Ease

Most people go to buy quality real estate investments at a fraction of the price outside of their market. Did you know, for example, that a California home of $400,000-$500,000 is equivalent to a Dallas, Little Rock, or Memphis home of $80,000? Did you know the rent can be as high as $1000 a month or more on a home?

Your competitors buy properties in these other markets, get a lot of cash flow for their capital, and quickly rack up a diverse asset portfolio. Are they geniuses? Are the investors in real estate better? The reply is no. Many of these people walked out of their comfort zone, risked very little, and are now reaping the rewards. How do they do this? Let's look at it.

1. Taking advantage of Markets–First, property investors in markets that, in many cases, had a significant price increase are struggling now that the appreciation is gone. Those markets ' savvy investors look outside and look for positive cash flow. Most markets within the U.S., especially the South, are not just growing markets, but have been running low prices for

quite a while. Look where there are economic growth and low prices. Example: Little Rock, Atlanta, Memphis, Houston, Birmingham, Montgomery, and others.

2. Do your homework-look online and find local groups for investment in real estate. Search for your target market partnerships. See if you can access their websites ' forums section. Who are the shakers and movers? What buys and sells a lot of real estate? Then look at other pages on the same platform such as Craigslist. Do you see any correspondence? Repeat titles, identical transactions, etc. should be seen. Use this knowledge to begin evaluating homes. Using Yahoo, Facebook, MSN, and others as well. For example: if you google the following, what sample city, real estate investment, or sample city discount properties would surface. Search for credible land sale firms. Stay away if they do not have an existing website. Those who are usually showing a guy don't have an excellent support team.

3. Survey to build a real estate investment team-Make a list and survey them after you check online and find out who buys and sells a lot of real estates. Find out who is their staff support. Do this buyer and seller work with rehab crews in particular? How about businesses in management? Closing Attorneys or Agents of Escrow? Each of these or more should be interviewed by 3. Be frank with violence. If you can tap a team's expertise, it can be easy to own property outside of your city. Make sure your management companies are willing to work with real estate investors, property buyers, and so on. Tell people about each other's reputations.

4. Book a Trip — Take a trip to your new market to meet your staff, go out into the streets, look at the properties available, and see the office for everyone. This is always going to be the real check. Creating a fake front online or the front on the phone is simple, but it's tough to cover up after show at their doorstep. Use the business for three days. Look at the wholesalers or agents working in all the communities. Make sure they won't give you areas of conflict. Tell them about rent rates, projections of recovery, rental time, etc. Test these figures with the supervisors and contractors. If all checks are done, go ahead. The right people's team is coming to light.

5. Buy and begin slowly. Most people are going to try to force you one time to buy many properties. Inside the risk range by property or two and see how it works. If it does the right thing: wash, rinse, and repeat. You've found a new investment opportunity for real estate! Perhaps you've had some fun exploring a new area as well.

By using you too, you will benefit from developments in real estate taking place throughout the US in undervalued markets.

How To Be The Real Estate Mogul

People who are considered to be moguls of real estate have not been born like that, even though they have grown up in a family of other successful investors. It's easy to assume that some people have just a talent to buy an investment property, or that it's out of reach for the abilities of the average person. It may be too much, in fact, for the patience of the average person, but never their skills.

It indicates very affirmatively that anyone who thinks about it can become a successful investor in real estate. That means there is no unique gene investing in real estate, without which the average person is doomed to misery or life below average. This means there's hope!

Merely observing a process is the best way to learn about investing in real estate. In the study of how to invest in real estate, there is a step-by-step method. The first step is to educate yourself about the parts of investment in real estate.

It essentially means that understanding what is referred to as the language of investment in real estate is imperative. We need to be able to select investments that will do well in the market to be successful in investing. To choose properties that will work optimally, it is necessary to read the records of the property. And to do any harm, these documents should be known. These documents are the property's accounting history. As a result, the prospective investor in real estate needs to learn finance and accounting. She doesn't need to become an authority either to hire an accountant for that kind of experience one day, but she must consider what her accountant communicates to her when they discuss it. To make wise choices, she will learn what the jargon means. It should be possible for her to grasp the materials and to infer what they mean to her.

She also has to do this with other real estate investment fields as well as learning enough real estate law to get through and learn about the buildings themselves. That's an excellent place to start. Once the aspiring investor masters finance, law, and property itself, she now has a foundation for educating herself about the markets. Now she can understand how location can influence a specific property's value, that even a beautiful building in an unfortunate part of the city is doomed to pick up just low rent. She can find out how to choose a demographic in which to buy properties, how to conduct research, and to whom to speak.

When she checks out a prospective house, the novice investor will return to what she has heard about banking, law, and apartments. She should have learned at some point which aspects of the potential property to be inspected, and that is much more than the structure itself. She will, of course, go over it with her professional inspector to determine the physical shape of the property. Still, she will even need to find some suitable management landscapers, business, and anyone who have link with the investment. She will know exactly how much it will cost to keep the place running until she makes a choice. She's going to know what the problems are and how much she's likely to benefit. She's going to know what it's doing now, what it's going to do now, and what it's going to do in the future.

She also knows that the intelligent investor is not attached to the idea of closing the purchase. Most deals are not supposed to be terminated, she knows. She understands, or she will appreciate that investing in real estate is mostly about research if she is to become successful. It's about tons of questions being searched and asked.

It is continuously carrying out the process that creates a real estate mogul. The trained investor in real estate is not going to do things unintelligently. She is continually on top of the marketplace and its assets activities.

If she does not perform well with an investment she owns, she knows this and acts accordingly.

In short, the real estate investor is transformed into a real estate mogul just by keeping himself well versed and continually learning. And by repetition, too.

CHAPTER TWO
Best Places to Buy Real Estate

Real Estate Facts There are various U.S. regions that are virtually hotbed for excellent rental properties of quality. In the course of time, homeownership aspirations have vanished, as this can be strongly correlated with the marked economic change. Consequently, many families are willing to settle for a rental property. And that's why it's time to embark on the real estate market with great opportunities. Homeowners will usually buy and sell homes for a profit. But these days, actually purchasing a home and renting the house may be more lucrative. Rental vacancies have dropped slightly across the U.S., reflecting the growing popularity of rental properties.

Statistically speaking, 1 in every 70 homes in the city of Las Vegas is entering a state of foreclosure. In addition, rent in this area is declining dramatically due to the decline in the housing market. If there has ever been a good time to invest in properties in Las Vegas, that's right now. When specific housing markets (such as this one) are in a recovery phase, capitalizing on them is important while there is still time. If you buy the homes while their value is shallow, you can cash in once their value has been restored to their average balance. Another excellent place for new home buyers in Orlando, Florida, which is characterized by prices of housing that have fallen over time. These homes are affordable and are located in an enviable, tropical environment.

Colorado Springs, another Great Housing Markets, is an untapped market that many aspiring homeowners are losing sight of. The median prices of housing in this city are meager. If you really want to take advantage of the housing market, consider investing in houses in Memphis, Tennessee. Housing prices in this region have dropped substantially, and there is always a lot to do with many festivals and other events in its busy streets. Florida, is another excellent location in Florida, offering a variety of housing options. You can expect to rent it out to eager occupants if you buy a property in this region. Houston, Texas, is another ideal home location. Besides being located in this big city's vast expanse, just under 300 miles from the Fort Worth real estate market, there is a lot of potential for home building in this area. In this particular region of Texas, there are very few restrictions on home construction.

Atlanta is one of the best places to buy the property and then rent out your property. This sprawling city is characterized by an unlike any other booming business atmosphere and is made up of international business people from all over the world. In addition, Columbus, Ohio, is a great place to buy land. Phoenix, however, has enormous potential in the housing market in Arizona. Housing prices are always reasonable due to its extreme climate. That's why you can hope to cash in on a home at a low cost, and you'll also find tenants. Therefore, remember the details mentioned above, before you invest your money in a home.

BUY REAL ESTATE

Buying a new house is often the most significant financial outlay in your whole life. With that in mind, the first time you can make the best decision is absolutely imperative. When you use these guidelines, there is higher chance that the figure-six outlay of purchasing a house will not be regretted.

Once you buy a lot of homes, even if you love the first property, you're visiting. The idea of buying a house and then, ultimately, the first property you see can be easy to fall in love with. Make sure to visit many other features for reference, just to make sure you have everything you want or need in the house you want.

Fall that helps you get a good idea of how well care has been taken over the years for the home you are considering buying. Take the gutters for a minute to look at. If the leaves leak out of them, you'll know they didn't take the time to clean them up. If they don't take the time for that simple maintenance, they may have neglected the other things in the home.

Have a good friend look at the house and tour the neighborhood before you buy a house because they may see things you don't. It's easy to get carried away with all the excitement and stress of finding a new home and miss things. Getting optimistic eyes to assess your house, neighborhood, and other variables that are personally relevant to you can prevent severe down the road problems.

The place is a significant part of the selection process for real estate. Look into the surrounding areas just as much as you do the home features. Find out how long you will have to travel to work from a distance. Get shopping, police, pharmacies and doctor's offices, daycare and colleges, and traffic and parking data to make sure it's convenient for your family.

Try out a few open houses when you're looking to buy your next home. Open Houses will give you an excellent opportunity to see what's available in a neighborhood, see different floor plans, meet with real estate agents, and get ideas to decorate or update. In the local Sunday paper, open house listings are readily available.

It is better to use your time when working with an agent to buy a home to sit down with the agent first and discuss what you're looking for. If they don't know what it is, how can they find a home that suits you?

Discount brokers can be something to consider when you're buying a house when you have time to do the research on the leg. They're much cheaper than a conventional broker, but they're doing much less for you. It will be your responsibility to set up appointments to see homes and write your own sales contract. You are going to save money, but you are going to work harder.

Buying real estate property is a tricky business, especially when you buy. Buying property is a significant decision, and you should be very cautious about who you are going to hire when looking for a real estate agent. You don't want your money to end up getting wasted. Find someone with a reference and do your research in advance.

People buying property to really make a home need to think about anything on a lengthy-term basis, including growing up children, energy cost changes, potential home upgrades, and much more. When you plan to buy a home, be a long-term thinker. This is definitely going to help you limit your mistakes.

From the receipt of an appraisal and inspection to the closure of the loan, the process of real estate is complicated and full of potential pitfalls. That's why every step of the way is essential to have guidance. Use these tips to simplify and manage the real estate buying process.

Best Time to Buy Real Estate

Whether for the very first time you are just investing or you have a significant level of the real estate experience in situation, you may find it very difficult always to know the real estate investment. Because this is the selling cost of the belonging is not the same. This continues to fluctuate from time to time. There are, however, several metrics that can help you know the best time to buy.

Economy recession During the economic slowdown, one of the most appropriate times for commercial real estate investment. The explanation is quite clear. There will be a lot of laying-off and unemployment as a result of the economic slowdown. In turn, this increase in unemployment will force several homeowners to desert their property and go to some other promising job area.

As a result, they look forward to selling off their homes as soon as possible and moving on to some new property. This urgency of theirs can make them even at a lower cost to sell their property.

Rise in interest rates Another great time measure depending on the investment in real estate to buy property is when interest rates rise. This is because higher interest rates will make it quite expensive to buy a new home. As a result, fewer people will choose to purchase the property.

Ultimately, if there are fewer buyers, house prices will fall to attract more buyers. So at a lower price, you can expect to buy a property. However, only your monthly mortgage payments will be higher in this case, but this will also be alone for a short period of time. This is because you can choose to refinance the mortgage for a low-interest rate once the interest rates drop again. This will result in the bank being paid less on a monthly basis.

Holidays According to the holidays of several real estate investment firms, going shopping for a home is the best time. This is the fact that the retailers, shops, and malls are providing multiple mega sales during holidays to draw customers. So this is where most people will focus on buying property and pay less attention. As a result, there will be fewer buyers, and home sales will fall automatically. This, in turn, will cause to a fall in property prices. As such, you can always take advantage of the vacation sales offers to invest property rentals.

And these are some of the vital indicators that can really help you find the right for real estate investment. Happy to invest!

THE BEST TIME TO BUY REAL ESTATE

Do you think that investing in real estate is not a good time? Think about it again! A combination of factors is now in harmony, making this market one of the strongest for real estate investment in recent history.

Investments are springing back into the Market-Yes, for the past year and a half, several investors were on the sideline, sitting on their cash and waiting for signs of life. However, signs of life are going to appear everywhere, and now is the time to come back on the business, while still low prices are unlikely to go any lower-real estate prices have reached the bottom in most areas, and the only path they can go is up. Once again, the smartest investors are taking good deals. What does all this mean for investors like you in real estate? More opportunities to make enormous profits.

Banks want to get rid of FAST properties–Although foreclosure rates are slowing down, and the housing market is springing back to life, banks have not yet processed all of their foreclosure properties. They're looking for these assets to unload-fast!

Low-interest rates-interest rates have fallen again and may fall even further. Prices are coming back down as more money is being pumped into housing by government programs, and banks are trying to get their cashback to work.

Tax credits— Congress agreed to extend the allowance of the first home buyer. This stimulates a new round of buying and selling, creating even more opportunities for investors.

The recession is still creating opportunities.

We still feel a terrible recession's effects. List numbers of people hunkering down and waiting for the economic woes storm to pass over the last year. And many of the experts and self-proclaimed experts out there tell us that buying and investing in real estate is a risky time.

It's just not true. When you find the right deal, it's always a good time to buy real estate. The real estate tycoons know this, and that's why they're in a big way on the market. And that's why the smart money is now investing in real estate, particularly now that it looks like we're coming out of recession.

The recession means more shutdowns.

The long lines of unemployment we see on the evening news are filled with something else: highly successful people in three-piece suits who never dreamed that they would end up unemployed. And what's worse, there are many of them facing hiccups.

Financial difficulties will force family members into smaller, more affordable homes, townhomes, or houses from the conveniences of an overpriced home. It ensures that housing will have enormous benefits as some families move down the ladder of the property, and others step up.

This gives a lot of opportunities for profit to the investment buyer. There will be not only more short sales, but also opportunities to work with homeowners who just want to get away from the stress and burden of having a home they can't afford anymore.

So when's the time to be an investor in real estate? Just now!

Make Millions Buying Real Estate

Have you heard of the issue of the Subprime mortgage? What about the bubble of real estate? If not, you've got to crawl out of the rock you've been living in and turn on the television or read a paper! Or perhaps the best thing you don't do is. Pair sub-prime mortgages with the Bubble real estate and the media will make all of us believe the world is coming to an end. It's crazy what the media chooses to focus on when there's a lack of tragedy or global travesty.

Although it is true that perhaps the lending industry has new restrictions when it comes to sub-prime lenders (people with less than perfect credit and very little cash down), we need to assess what impact this has on the real estate market. While liar loans have been removed as they have come to be known, or reported income or declared properties, FHA is still going strong. Indeed, as first-time home buyers seek alternative loans, these loans have increased dramatically. This program depends much less on credit scores. This makes the use of one of the many services currently available for down payment assistance.

However, as you examine what proportion of loans are actually made to sub-prime lenders, you continue to see that this is a smaller number than the news reports. The sub-prime situation is not as catastrophic as we would like to trust in the media. What are you saying? Do you mean to tell me the truth has been exaggerated by the media? Would this be the first time information is distorted in order to bring a "story?"

So what's really causing the real estate market to slow down? Above all, we are built over. Country-wide builders have churned out new homes faster than they can sell. The builders made a fortune selling new homes due to massive demand and the willingness of consumers to access financing at will. As these homes started saturating communities across the U.S. and lenders continued to tighten controls, investors began drying up. The builders were understandably unwilling to give up their cash cow.

With increased vigor, they continued to produce these houses, almost like a factory assembly line. To buy the new builds, buyers needed to sell their existing homes. This started to create a fake lull in the property market. All of a sudden, excess inventory entered the markets. In areas where many jobs are being created, there has been a dramatic increase in home inventories. It actually fuelled these slowdowns in combination with the media doomsday report and "created" a real problem.

The next crucial element is the country-wide record number of foreclosures. The same lenders who now tighten their rules gave mortgages to anyone who was willing to fog a mirror. They put investors in these teaser loans or flexible mortgage rates to top it off. These were temporary low rates, which were adjusted after a specified period of time (usually 2-5 years). Once these prices have been changed, consumers notice the payment there has doubled and tripled at times! Could you imagine that you can only qualify for the monthly payment given to you on this "teaser" rate to accelerate your salary after the adjustment? There's no wonder so many foreclosures.

This is the next question. Where do these foreclosures end when the bank takes them back? You've guessed that. They stay right in the beautiful neighborhood where they've always been. But what do you think? The bank writes off a portion of its loss and brings it back on the market, sometimes at a considerable discount (usually much lower than comparable neighborhood home sales). What is the use of assessors to determine the value of a home? Similar sales of recent years? That's okay. These foreclosures all of a sudden become the comparable new sales, and that is the beginning of a neighborhood's decline in value.

What can we do with this situation now? We need to purchase such homes as owners, creditors, or homebuyers before they go into foreclosure.

If you don't buy until foreclosure, after the selling of foreclosure, you can still pick up amazing offers! Well now you're saying (to the media's chagrin) why would you buy now, you're just saying the value of homes is falling? It should know that you need to buy when everyone else is selling. You need to be selling when everyone is buying. Do you see this logic? If you're one of the few buyers in a buyers market that you're looking for, you can set your own terms and prices on a particular property or move to the next. You want to be in the drivers ' seat to put yourself.

If the market is saturated with inventory, there are a lot of motivated sellers willing to be much more flexible than we just came out of during the seller's market. You have a lot more opportunities to buy property at a substantial discount or first terms. Can't stress enough that you need to purchase all the property that you can buy right now. During the downturn, millionaires were made. How are you asking? Because those in opposition were willing to find an opening.

Looking at a graph that shows the prices of real estate starting in 1900, the overall big picture shows a marked increase over the years. There are up and down with the way, but the values have always risen in view of the big picture. If history keeps repeating itself and offering a look into the future, it's time to buy, buy, buy! Most experts agree that within the next 18-24 months, the real estate market will correct itself.

It gives the general public an unfair advantage. If ever there was a time to step out and take a calculated risk, it's time now! Just think about how you can put yourself if you hold multiple assets that unexpectedly rise dramatically due to supply and demand when the market turns around (and it will). Don't be one of the crowds to the detriment of the government. Don't miss this opportunity. Be one of the few who take advantage of and succeed in the opportunities set before you.

What to Look For When Buying Real ESTATE?

During recession, when you go real estate shopping, you can almost sure that you buy, you will get profit. Some of the places take time to be impacted when a recession hits, but later or sooner, any area can begin to pinch- you can stick a pin in the map as you try to decide where to make your investment.

Of course, even if you can make a profit almost anywhere doesn't mean you shouldn't take action to maximize that benefit. Would you go for the Godiva candy or the M&Ms if you were sitting in the middle of a giant room with treats that were yours to take free? If you have the option between such a property you're going to make a small investment on and a property you're going to make a fantastic profit on when the economy starts to rise again, go to the property you're going to get the highest return!

Where will you find the best deals? Urban properties and residences are often more in demand in the suburbs of these metropolitan areas than those requiring a long commute to get to the basics of life. Homes in Washington, D.C. suburbs in a small town like Rexville, NY, they're going to sell for a higher profit (and much faster) than a home. (Do not even think too hard if you have never heard of it— most of the rest of the world hasn't!) When you start investing first, it's usually recommended that you pick up property close to home, where you know the neighborhood, the general atmosphere, and, most importantly, what you're selling! This is particularly essential if you select to do your restoration, as many areas in the country are highly respected for their historical value, and that will result in a much lower return on your investment if they have been stripped and decked out in the latest style than if they have been carefully restored. An experienced rehabber will know this. It won't be a starting investor.

Some other factors that you may have to consider before you close the deal are:

- Neighborhood quality. Sadly, there are slums in all urban areas. An environment with a high murder rate, a large amount of vandalism and damage to property, regular drug abuse and constant police investigations will be much less attractive for a prospective buyer than a home situation in a safer part of the city, where they can comfortably allow their kids to walk out of the front door without having to worry they won't come home.
- The house's state. There were several, most investors who plunged right into the real estate and rehabilitation world and bought a handyman's exclusive only to discover that by the time they paid for the property's repairs, the profit margin was significantly lower than they hoped for and what they would have made investing in an estate that needed a little less work.

Take the time to carefully inspect the home before you commit to buying a property. Some factors will be both challenging and expensive to fix, such as a leaky roof, faulty foundation, termites, and extensive mold. Unless you can get the property for a song, justifying the amount of time and expense you're going to spend on the restoration project, it might be best to let that one pass you by.

- After that, what you want to do with it. This is probably the most significant factor when it comes to investing in real estate because what you intend to do with the property after you buy it makes all the difference when you decide which property types are appropriate and what are not. If you are planning to rehabilitate a property, then reselling it as a single-family residence may be a perfectly profitable proposition to buy a small ranch house on the edge of town. You will probably be able to sell more than you paid for the property and justify the investment.

If you arrange to rent out the property, you will want to investigate the neighborhood's current rent rates before you can determine the investment's success with any degree of accuracy. There are some areas where income-based housing pushes down the neighborhood's average rental price, which is good news for renters but could lead to significant inconvenience for the investor who has paid hundreds of thousands of dollars for a property they will only be able to rent for a few hundred dollars a month.

Our story's moral? Take the time to understand your options carefully and do your homework before you close the deal, no matter how attractive the offer may be.

If you've invested in real estate for the past ten years, of course, none of this is news for you! Experienced investors who are familiar with market trends and identify weaknesses in potential properties will find a tempting proposition spreading the buffet of low-priced real estate before them, and reaching beyond their immediate demographic boundaries may offer a new wealth of opportunities for tremendous profit gain.

Just remember that investing in a recession is slightly different from investing in a booming economy. You're going to hear me repeatedly saying this because it can't be stressed enough-when you're investing in real estate during a recession, you're investing in the long run. Many of today's real estate investors have made their fortune on the market by taking advantage of the "Then, Now, Now!" mindset of today and buying in and disposing of real estate in a short time. When the economy is strong, it's not at all uncommon for an ambitious buyer to be able to buy and flip a property in less than a month in the space of a weekly rehabber. Any property you invest in during a recession may remain in your hands for several months before you can earn a maximum return, as the entire investment point during a downturn is to buy an asset at the lowest possible price and sell it when the economy goes back up.

It's rare for the knowledgeable investor to find themselves in this circumstance. Still, it's entirely possible for spread too thin when there was just too much to resist the temptation of pages on pages of available property. Suddenly, they are not only responsible for the amount they paid to buy the property in the first place for the initial investment but also for the taxes, rehabilitation, and maintenance required to maintain it and prepare it for sale.

Try to limit yourself to what you can afford in the long run with a realistic expectation. If, as the recession continues, you find that you have more than enough capital in your hand to pick up a couple more properties, you always have that option, but disposing of a property that you can't afford during a recession can be harder than taking a submarine and diving for Atlantis, which is why investing in real estate during a recession is so lucrative to start with.

Tips when Buying Real Estate!

Real estate continues to be a substantial investment in many areas in today's financial climate. In the real estate market, educated buyers will always make the most of it. These top real estate purchase tips will help you enter confidently into your next real estate transaction.

- Look for the right agent!

It's invaluable to hire the right real estate agent. The realtor you choose is your guide to important information about schools, zoning, city and county laws, neighborhood trends, building and remodeling and rental restrictions, and property values if you are unfamiliar with the area. Each municipality has different laws governing what a property can and cannot do. Sanibel is one of America's most beautiful cities due in part to its strict building codes and urban planning. Having knowledge many aspects of real estate transactions on a personal level, the buyers and sellers understand situations and concerns. For years, he was an island property owner and went through several deals in local real estate. From buying and selling lots to building new homes with local builders to investing in property-producing rental income and using 1031 tax-free exchanges, don't just sell island real estate; invest in it because there's no place like Sanibel and Captiva in the world. Whether you're dealing with me or someone else, it's essential to find the right realtor.

- Use 1031 exchanges of taxes and save money!

1031 Investment property exchanges are tax-free exchanges. Internal Revenue Code Section 1031 is one of the last major tax shelters. If you purchase a "like-kind" investment property within 180 days of a similar type of property being sold and you are willing to increase the amount of the property's debt or value, your capital gains taxes can be deferred ultimately. Understand 1031 tax exchanges and how to take advantage of them for your financial benefit. Keep in mind that a qualified intermediary must have acted by a neutral party. You can also buy and sell real estate through your self-directed retirement account.

- Financing pre-qualification!

Prequalifying for a loan may not seem so crucial until, at the same time, as another buyer, you find your perfect paradise property. When a property is priced for sale, more than one buyer will usually be attracted. As a seller receives an offer, the two most vital things they take into consideration are the price and contingencies. A contract contingent on the purchaser to obtain funding makes them uncomfortable with the offer for some sellers. Remove any doubt in a seller's mind by prequalifying for the sum you will spend on buying any house. This is particularly important if you unexpectedly have a price reduction in your dreamland. Could other buyers come into the picture when this happens, they didn't look at the property before it went "On Sale!" Often a seller will take over a higher offer with a financially stable contract. Be ready to make a deal!

- Site, Site, Location!

"Location, location, location" is still, and should always be, a huge consideration for you as the buyer while being overused as a phrase for real estate! If you are bothered by something about the location of a property, be aware that any buyer you hope to attract when and if you need to resell the property will be bothered by the same location disadvantage! It's important to ask a lot of questions, but if you're not familiar with the culture, it's often hard to know the right questions to ask. That's why choosing and hiring the right real estate agent to represent your interests when purchasing a property is so valuable.

- Have a home check!

Having an inspection report from a licensed professional building inspector of your choosing will protect you from many hidden defects. Why are you playing with such a significant investment in finance? Let a professional inspector point out areas that are not obvious to be fixed or replaced. A good inspector will get you with a lengthy report covering all home systems from electrical, plumbing, roofing, and structural issues. Once you have received a story, you can start negotiations about repairs again. Up to a specified financial amount, a seller will often agree to make necessary repairs. When a seller lists their property "as it is," they let you know they don't want to fix or replace any part of the property. If you're interested in an "as is" property and you're not going to level the structure and build new ones, it's still in your best interest to get a report of the inspection. Don't look for termites and some problems of pest that are harmful with the building inspector. Although pest damage will be seen by an inspector, it is best to separate termite inspection carried out by a licensed company that understands and can eliminate pests.

- Get an insurance survey and description!

Surveys will show a property's easements, invasions, and boundary lines. You are assured that the property limit lines have been maintained by surveying a home in an established neighborhood. When homeowners build walls, sheds, decks, garages, and other structures to their properties over time, it is possible to cross boundary lines putting part of their construction on your land, or other way round.

Title Insurance will cover your investment in your property from another party claiming ownership interest. Searches title will reveal links placed by vendors on a feature, or errors in previous title transfers. When in the backstretch of a deal, the final thing you need to find is obligations on property like easements, undisclosed owners, tax liens, or leases. If a claim arises after a property has been purchased, there is a title insurance company to protect your ownership interest in the park.

- Be true!

When it comes to property features, Wants and Needs are very different. If every home you see has the quality you want, but the price range you need exceeds. Let's be realistic. Who wouldn't enjoy a large beachfront home or condominium with all the bells and whistles, competently decorated? It's always fun to look at properties that exceed your price range, but it can be extremely frustrating and upsetting. Look realistically at the price range you "need," keeping an eye on that individual property that has the potential to evolve into the dream home you "want." Look at the home's architecture always beyond the wallpaper, floor coverings and furnishings; it is then you will find potential properties.

- Wisely use contractual contingencies!

In a contract to buy a house, contingencies are designed to protect you, the buyer! This may seem dumb to say, but it is essential to remember that you need to negotiate with the seller in order to reach an agreement. The seller is required to have reasonable contingencies to a bid. Construction inspections, termite and pest inspections, funding, and surveys are typical contingencies. Most transactions are split over small details, and problems are easy to fix. Note that their property is emotional to sellers. If you can see that it is necessary to make significant repairs or replacements due to negligence or age, make allowances in your offer price for this. All things are negotiable is still valid unless you are so disturbing the seller that they refuse to work with you. Try not to list cosmetic changes as contingencies that you would like the seller to make. When writing a contract, cosmetic changes are subjective, be objective.

- Understand the issues of regional health and safety!

A knowledgeable realtor will help you understand other concerns related to health and safety that should be addressed when buying a property. Topics of safety and health may include EIFS (Synthetic Stucco), air quality indoors, radon, mold, and lead paint.

- Request Info!

Don't be afraid. Ask them for information when you've hired a realtor to work for you. Would you like to see all the properties in your price range, the features you need, or just the houses that a realtor wants you to see? You deserve all the data you need to make a decision that is educated. Do you imagine buying the home you thought was right for your kids, just to find that you never got information about a similar property suitable for all your needs?

CHAPTER THREE
Buying Real Estate In Different Countries

BUY REAL ESTATE IN HAMPTON

Patrick's been serving in the army at St. Monroe in Hampton, VA. With his wife Janie and two children, he lived off base in a nearby apartment. The bottom is on the water, and there he loved fishing. He received military orders overseas, and for two years, the family went to Korea. At the end of that tour, he was stationed at Ft. Eustis is located in Newport News, VA, just 18 miles from Ft. Franklin, Monroe. He quickly came back from his favorite pier to his fishing routine. He enjoyed the area so much that he decided to keep the family here and purchased a home in neighboring York County, VA. It is meant to give an explanation of why so many people, both military and civilian, chose to stay and buy homes in Norfolk, Newport News, York County, and Williamsburg, Virginia.

These cities are part of a larger regional metropolitan area that consists of other significant towns divided by water into two sides. Formerly understand as, and sometimes still mean to as, this larger land area is called Hampton Roads. It is divided into two teams by water, all of which are considered local. One side has a few well-known cities such as Norfolk, and the Southside is called Virginia Beach. And the other is known as the Virginia Peninsula, the subject of this. Hampton, Newport News, York County and Williamsburg are among the major cities.

HAMPTON: Hampton City is located between Williamsburg and the Southside Bridge-Tunnel to Norfolk & VA Beach. Hampton real estate is home to a number of major employers such as Fort Monroe, Langley Air Force Base, and the aeronautical research facility NASA Langley Research Center. Yet there's also plenty of arts and culture. The Phoebus community downtown in the city boasts a rich history of arts, entertainment, and architecture. And regular events such as the Langley Speedway NASCAR races and live music at the parks and the annual Hampton Jazz Festival are common among both property owners and tourists.

Due to its numerous higher education schools and institutions, including Hampton University and Thomas Nelson Community College, many families are attracted to live and buy homes in Hampton. Others are drawn to Hampton real estate due to the proximity of the city to its city beaches, such as Buckroe and the world-renowned VA Beach, about a 40-minute drive away. There are many other job opportunities as well as shopping for residents of Hampton. The city has taxes from homeowners that are very reasonable.

NEWPORT NEWS: A city line divides Hampton and Newport News. Newport News real estate is situated on the James River's north shore, where the Chesapeake Bay meets the river. The town was built in the early 1600s. Newport News real estate today features two historic communities, Hilton Village and North End / Huntington Heights, both listed on the Historic Places National Register. For fun, visitors and homeowners alike can enjoy a wide range of activities at Newport News Park, which includes two golf courses in its 8,000 acres. Newport News is undergoing a renewal, attracting even more homebuyers to real estate in Newport News. Because it is also surrounded by water on the Peninsula, many enjoy the lifestyle of the waterfront and the mild climate offered by the location of the city along the James River. Others are attracted to Newport News real estate due to the job opportunities to the town, including a significant shipbuilder and military facilities. Newport News also has higher education centers, several shopping areas, and a high-tech research center.

YORK COUNTY: One of the eight original counties of Virginia was created in 1634. Its 108 square miles now serve as a tranquil and relaxing community. Hampton and Newport News are the nearby cities. This makes real estate in York County an attractive choice for those moving to these areas. The economy of the county is linked to the sizeable military-industrial complex that characterizes the whole area of Hampton Roads. It still maintains its early maritime roots, however. Shipbuilding and processing of seafood continue to thrive along the rivers, James and York. And with the combined shorelines of the rivers running for over 200 miles, real estate in York County remains an ideal choice for water-lovers.

York County real estate, along with Williamsburg and Jamestown, is part of Virginia's Historic Triangle. Yorktown city is located at the Colonial Parkway's northern point. This is a scenic route that connects the Historic Triangle's three locations. The ten elementary schools, four middle schools, and seven high schools serving the youths of the county attract many families to York County real estate. Others buy real estate from York County due to the county's scenic nature, fair weather, and relatively low living costs.

WILLIAMSBURG: Nothing in the city beats Williamsburg when it comes to major attractions. The town is a great place to buy land. The city is known as a resident and homeowner's high-end community. It's almost 12,000 in total. But this is small compared to Colonial Williamsburg's 4 million sightseers a year. The attraction is an interactive restoration of the original capital of the state and life of Virginia's early settlers, who were among the first to settle the nation. Other popular destinations in Williamsburg include theme park Busch Gardens, Water County USA, Jamestown, Yorktown, Williamsburg Winery, and outlet shopping centers in the city.

This was an overview of the Virginia Peninsula's significant cities. The Peninsula has a mild climate of four seasons. This means that you can enjoy outdoor activities throughout the year. The weather is temperate and seasonal in the Hampton Roads area. Summers with cool evenings are hot and humid. The average annual temperature is 70 ° F, with a yearly average 6-inch winter snowfall and an average 47-inch annual rainfall. This makes it an excellent place for all people looking to escape the brutal winters to relocate from north to north. And for people out west looking to escape the summers of the desert, it's also a great choice.

The waterways known as Hampton Roads are one of the largest natural harbors in the world, incorporating the James River and Elizabeth River mouths with many smaller rivers and flowing into the Chesapeake Bay close its mouth, leading to the Atlantic Ocean. This is at the center of the Virginia

Peninsula and Southside Hampton Roads' main attraction. It's boaters, fishermen, and haven for beachgoers. Forget Florida or California, with the exception of palm trees and the high cost of living, the Peninsula and Hampton Roads have everything they have.

There are a variety of higher education options, such as Hampton University, and Thomas Nelson Community College serves as the college community. Newport News includes a public university, Christopher Newport University. Other public universities in the vicinity include Old Dominion University, Norfolk State University, and William and Mary College.

Two airports are serving this metro area. Newport News / Williamsburg International Airport, Newport News, and Southside's Norfolk International Airport. The Newport News / Williamsburg International Airport, however, is the primary for the Virginia Peninsula. The airport has a historic fourth year of double-digit growth, making it one of the country's fastest-growing airports. At present, the airport has seven airlines providing nonstop services across the country to twenty-five destinations.

A regional bus service called Hampton Roads Transit provides public transportation on the Peninsula, the Southside, and throughout Hampton Roads. The Peninsula's main thoroughfares are Mercury Blvd, which stretches Hampton's length and once had the most restaurants and restaurants across the country. The other is Jefferson Ave running Newport News' entire range. The I-64 and I-664 interstate system serves the entire Hampton Roads area as the primary way of traveling back and forth between the Peninsula and Southside to VA Beach.

In closing, the Hampton Roads area has recently been voted one of the country's best places to live. Due to a high military presence, including the Army, Navy, Air Force, Marines, and Coast Guard, the region remains a popular retirement destination. This is also why the city has experienced some relief from some of the economy's economic downturns, including the housing market. It is also well below the national average when it comes to crime and unemployment rates compared with cities with an equal population.

Besides the beautiful landscape surrounded by water and the miles of waterfront property, this is all. The culture is vibrant, and the nightlife is lively. Whether you're here for business or pleasure, there's everything about the Virginia Peninsula and the Greater Hampton Roads.

CONSIDERATIONS IN BUYING REAL ESTATE AND MOVING TO COSTA RICA

Buying Real Estate Strategy in Costa Rica When we settled on Costa Rica, the destination we planned to retire to the first thing we did was to develop a strategy to find a piece of property that met our size, location, and budget requirements. We were pretty knowledgeable shoppers who bought and sold nearly a dozen state properties, so we thought we knew what we were doing. We were looking for a property in Costa Rica. We realized there wasn't foreclosed homes much in Costa Rica's way, as most homes don't have a mortgage, most of which were acquired for cash in the past. Costa Rica's mortgage market is still in its infancy. You can't typically get a mortgage on land, only funding from developers. The developer holds the note in this type of financing. Leases usually require large down payments in Costa Rica for finished homes or building mortgages. Costa Rican banks want at least 20 percent of the mortgage value as collateral. Luckily, usually, you can promise land that you own as collateral for a construction loan that is what many owners end up doing in our projects.

You do not need licensing to sell property in Costa Rica. As a consequence, if they think they can engage in a sale and make a profit, almost everyone will claim to be a realtor. Costa Rica also has no regional MLS program. Agreements for listing and commissioning are not standardized. Realtors do not act as an agent of "buyers" or an agent of "sellers." Most just hope to make a profit. Realtors are reluctant to share the list with realtors without a standard system of commissions and referral fees. That means most real estate developers will only show you their own listings in Costa Rica. Finding a Project Many Costa Rican real estate developers are new to the industry. What they will soon learn is that Costa Rica's development is highly regulated. It is a challenge to obtain permits to subdivide, construct roads, install water lines, or electricity. It boasts staunch conservation in

Costa Rica. For ventures targeted at North Americans and Europeans, the government has created new barriers in recent years to slow the growth of international development companies. Verify any developer's experience that you are considering. See what they've done, not what they're saying they're going to do. Visit the programs they have. Ask for fees, CC&As; and restrictions on deeds. In a certain amount of time, some developers need you to build. Some allow you to use their building services, even if they may have little or no experience. Find out what kind of development and titling they're doing as well. Are they offering limited-use and value agricultural parcels? Are they selling "Parcel Minima" plots with minimal utilities and few developer specifications to carry electricity, water, or roads to the lots? Is there a gated project? Gated projects also make it possible for developers to provide inside the gate little infrastructure and services. Once inside the gate, no municipal requirements are applied. Figure out what and when services will be offered prior to purchase. Choose what you see, not what they're going to tell you. Be vigilant of brochures full of artist's descriptions of what creation would look like. It is a prime example of Paragon Properties.

Determining Cost-Appraisals In the U.S., as part of the buying process, we are used to getting a property valuation completed. In Costa Rica, assessments are uncommon because mortgages on assets are less frequent, but they are becoming more common. The bank holding the mortgage demands most appraisals. Don't expect to have an evaluation done in Costa Rica or even find an appraiser. Be a judge of your own. Teach yourself. Kristina also took a complete set of courses that the Appraisal Institute offered cost thousands of dollars to learn how to make appraisals. Kristina was trying to gain additional expertise for an appraiser. Examinations have three parts; comps that are comparisons to similar property in the area with similar characteristics; revenue approach that looks at the income a property would provide from rentals or lease agreements; and construction costs that look at the expense of the raw land and any upgrades based on current construction costs. Unless explicitly stated otherwise, all evaluations in the states consist of all three approaches.

Past and Present Property Values Nearly every initiative in Costa Rica had been selling like hotcakes a few years ago. Prices rose with no end in sight. Condo prices were reaching $1200 per square meter in the central valley in cities like Escazu and Santa Ana, and some were topping $2000. Quality single-family home builders were in short supply, and the building waiting list was growing. Most of the major hotel chains and a slew of developers pounced to build condos on Costa Rica, realizing that 78 million baby boomers were already searching for options. Guanacaste, and especially the area around Costa Rica's Liberia International Airport, boomed with a high rise and low growth. Once considered a lowly surfing region, areas such as Jaco sprouted high-rise projects overnight. At the same time, builders such as Sonesta and Daystar started nine condo projects in Jaco. The crane is becoming a common sight, not the bird. Even as far south as Manuel Antonio, there was a breakthrough in high rise projects.

As the world economy contracted, the ShakeOut Then came the slowdown. Some projects were abandoned while others slowed down. Prices have down in these types of projects as well as insignificant developments of single-family homes built on the basis of speculation. Many of these builders have to keep selling some inventory to avoid bankruptcy. Banks were now pulling backload commitments once flushed with money.

Many buyers have been stuck with a partially completed project. Some developers went bankrupt, leaving the owners to compete with infrastructure. In many areas, the market has lost value, particularly in Guanacaste and the central Pacific region around Jaco. The best was done by the southern Pacific region. The height restriction of three stories (from Dominical South to Panama) has driven developers away from high-rise developments. Limited accessibility kept large projects out of the region, and there remained a low inventory of finished homes. Prices on raw land have dropped slightly without ocean views, but plots with ocean views have continued to rise in size.

Costa Rica has a two-tiered pricing system, that of Tico-style homes and North American-style homes in ex-pat communities. Many North Americans do not do well in Tico-style dwellings or neighborhoods in Tico, although some old hippies and so on may do so. Expat-oriented housing offers a variety of options. High-rise buildings with secure parking, upscale residential neighborhoods, large communities such as (expensive) Los Suenos golf developments, or small projects such as those from Jaco to Quepos dotting the coast. Further south, it is more difficult to find these forms of innovations.

Pacific Lots Our Pacific Lots project is by far the largest and oldest residential development in Costa Rica, but we are a single-family. Because we built only custom homes, we never had inventory that was unsold to glut the market. In the hills overlooking the ocean above the village of Ojochal below us, our developments spread. In the past few years, Uvita's neighboring town, just to our north, has become a large shopping center. Most of us in our village tend to be close to this commercial development and not right in town. We build houses in North American style, have no deadline, and if you don't want to use us, you are welcome to hire any other builder.

BUY REAL ESTATE IN CANADA

Why are you investing in Canada?

Canada is likely the world's most exceptional country and is often close to the top of the UN Life Quality Tables. Besides, Canada is a significant immigrant destination. These highly skilled and qualified individuals need accommodation when they land, so the demand for rental housing of good quality is likely to stay so better in future.

Realtors are brokering the bulk of real estate transactions. The Multiple Listing System is available to all licensed realtors. MLS is an enormous home database for sale across Canada. The advantage of MLS is that each realtor can search each other's listings, saving a tremendous amount of time and leather for shoes.

A growing number of owners choose to market their homes directly in addition to realtor listed properties, thus saving on realtor commissions. Small asking price in the form, the commission savings are often partially passed on. The downside is a higher degree of seller or buyer's expertise and work. Anyway, if you're looking for property in Canada, it's worth checking out the "For Sale By Owner" (FSBO) listings.

In deciding whether to make an offer, it is essential to look at actual selling property prices rather than merely asking for quotations. Sold prices are the price people want to pay for properties instead of what sellers are hoping to get. Realtors should be able to provide this detail, as opposed to seeing the Canadian House Prices.

Make sure look the strata by-laws for any restrictions on rentals, animals, other rulings for strata properties (see below). Buying a rental unit and then discovering and owners-only regulation wouldn't be proper.

Most apartments and condominiums, as well as some houses, are under strata. It essentially means that unit owners are creating type of company to control and operate the complex as a whole. In the case of large condominiums, the number of strata members will vary from a handful to hundreds or more.

Strata leaders annually elect from their number a strata council. The strata council effectively forms the complex's "government," negotiating maintenance contracts, creating and amending by-laws, imposing fines to criminals, etc. The strata as a whole are determining the significant issues.

For strata properties, there are two types of management, self-managed and professionally managed. In management costs, professional management is likely to cost more, which means that the job has been assigned, and owners can sit and forget it. Self-management is more natural but needs more hands-on participation from different members of the strata, e.g., notes will appear regularly asking volunteers for this or that. NB, the costs of management will not be significantly much in the case of broad strata as they will be spread across a larger number of units. You may prefer to go for professional management if you are not in watering lawns or painting areas.

In Canada, realtors should be qualified and licensed by the Provincial Association of Immobilities. As with any profession, individuals' quality varies, but they should all have the necessary skills and adhere to the code of conduct of their association. Realtor commission is not cheap for sellers, often on the first $100,000 in the region of seven percent and three percent on the rest. However, realtor services are free for buyers (being paid for by the seller. Using a (different) realtor is common for both sellers and buyers. As mentioned above, the realtors of the buyer are free of charge to the buyer (their money are paid from the commission of the selling realtor). A realtor buyer will be able to access all MLS listings and show you any number of selling agents listed properties. The buyer's realtor will assist you in writing an offer, and in any negotiations, should work for the buyer.

Choosing a realtor with local knowledge where you want to buy is essential. A good indicator is a personal recommendation. Otherwise, select from the numerous free real estate listings papers two or three realtors offering services to buyers. Give a call to them and choose the one with which they like they will work best. Buyers typically don't sign realtor's contracts, so if you don't get the level of attention, you don't expect, you shouldn't be afraid to change.

Making an offer The next step is to create a formal proposal to the seller after viewing a property that you decide you would like to own. We should be help with this if you are using a realtor. The offer indicates how much you are willing to pay for the property and the dates on which you wish to complete the transaction and obtain possession (NB the time of possession is usually one day after completion).

Usually, the offer also includes some conditions, such as subject to satisfactory inspection, and accounts, and approving copies of strata minutes obtaining funding, selling the current home, etc. Any conditions you want, you may add, but the more terms you have and the more stringent they are, the more likely your offer is to be refused by the seller-especially if you are looking for a significant reduction. The fewer provisions you have, of course, the more likely the seller is to drop the price significantly.

Be sure to make the sight and acceptance of strata minutes, accounts, and by-laws a condition of your bid if you are seeking a stratum managed house. One thing that needs to be checked is that the levels have enough cash in their accounts. This is money to be used in case significant works such as repairs to the roof are needed.

One way to avoid a financial condition is to talk to lenders about how much funding is available in advance. By theory, you should be able to obtain an arrangement, but typically a lender will want to carry out a property appraisal to ensure their capital's protection.

The seller accepts the bid, refuses it, or gives a counteroffer (such as a discount between your offer and the price you ask). We may also seek to change other aspects of the deal, such as the dates of completion and ownership.

The buyer should endeavor to remove his or her conditions once an offer has been accepted.

Property inspection Before finalizing your bid, you will most likely want the property to be professionally inspected. The way to find an inspector is on personal recommendation, refusing to ensure that you are eligible for the role, e.g., by being a member of a respectable body such as the Home & Property Inspectors Association of Canada.

With your intended purchase, the inspection will almost certainly raise some issues. Don't be alarmed; these may indicate that your selected inspector is doing his job correctly. Ideally, the problems are minor, but if significant issues arise, you have several options: calculate the cost of fixing the problem(s) and adjust the offer accordingly. Put the seller's responsibility to solve the problem(s) with the requirement that they provide proof and guarantees for the work done. Remove from the deal. If your offer has been written correctly, you can do so freely. A lousy inspection report may result in a loss of contract, but it's much better than finding later that you bought a turkey.

Finalization of the purchase Once the inspection report is approved and the other conditions fulfill the purchase offer is finalized. A deposit is payable at this point, and the offer becomes binding. You will lose the deposit if you change your mind and can be sued as well.

Once your offer has been accepted, and all conditions have been fulfilled, you will need to hire an attorney to handle the transfer, i.e., the transfer of title from seller to buyer. Once again, a potent predictor is a personal recommendation. Otherwise, talk to many lawyers to get quotes. Do not merely go for the cheapest, but also consider how well the question has been handled.

The lawyer will also calculate the amount owed upon completion in addition to the transfer of title. This may include adjustments for property taxes, interest in utilities and mortgages, and any applicable tax on land transfer.

Start Residential Real Estate Investing

Investing in residential real estate is a business activity that has grown dramatically in popularity over the past couple of years. Ironically, there often seem to be a lot of individual jumping on board with investments such as stock, gold, and real estate as the market moves up and dropping off the car and pursuing other activities once the market slumps. It means a lot of real estate's investors are leaving money on the table in a way that's human nature.

Through knowing the nature of your markets for investment in residential real estate and behaving in contrast to the rest of the market, you can often make more money as long as you also stick to the principles of investment in real estate.

Investing in real estate, whether you are buying residential or commercial property, is not a scenario that is getting-rich-quick. Sure, if that's your bag, you can make some quick cash flipping houses, but it's a full-time business, not a passive, long-term investment. The word "investment" means you're committed to the prolonged haul activity. Often, that's just what it takes for real estate to make money.

So, when pundits are crying about the slump in the residential real estate market, and the speculators are wondering if that's the bottom line, let's go back to the fundamentals of investing in residential real estate and learn how to make a long-term investment in real estate, in good and bad markets.

A Return To The Fundamentals of Investing Residential Real Estate When a real estate goes up, up, up, it may seem easy to invest in real estate. All ships are rising with a rising tide, and you can still make money if you're in the right place at the right time, even if you've bought a deal with no equity and no cash flow.

Without much research and market knowledge, however, it's hard to time the market. A good strategy is to make sure you know the four residential real estate investment profit centers and make sure that all of them are taken into account by your next residential real estate investment deal.

Cashflow-How much money does the residential property bring in every month after the expenses have been paid? That seems to be easy to calculate if you know how much the rental income is and how much the mortgage is. However, once you take care of a rental property in everything else-things like vacant position, bills, maintenance and repairs, marketing, record keeping, legal fees, and the like - it really begins to add up.

Appreciation-Having the property goes up in value as long as you own it has historically been the most profitable part of owning property. However, as we have seen recently, the number of immobilities can also be DOWN. Leverage (in this case, your bank loan) is a double-edged sword. When you buy in an appreciating market, it can increase your rate of return, but it can also increase your rate of loss when the value of your property decreases. Plan to hold your place real estate investment property for at least five years for sensible, low-risk investment in real estate. This should give you the ability to predict market ups and downs so that you can see from a benefit point of view at a time when it makes sense.

Debt Pay down-Every month you make the bank's mortgage payment, a small portion of it will lower your loan's balance. Because of the mortgages way are structured, a loan that is typically amortized has a minimal amount of debt pay-down at the beginning, but if you manage to keep the loan in place for a number of years, you will see that as you approach the end of the loan term, more and more of your principle is being used to withdraw the debt. All this means, of course, that in the first place, you have an amortizing loan. If you have an interest-only mortgage, it will lower your payments, but you will not benefit from any investment down payments.

When you plan to hold the property for 5-7 years or longer, it makes sense to look at an interest-only loan, as the mortgage pay-down you can receive during that period is negligible, and it can benefit your cash flow to have an interest-only loan, as long as interest rate upward increases do not raise your payments faster than you planned and destroy your cash flow. If you plan to keep the property on a long-term basis, and you have a high-interest rate, it makes sense to get an accruing loan that will eventually reduce your investment loan's balance and make it go away. Make sure that you run the numbers on your investment strategy to see if it makes sense for you to get a loan at a fixed rate of interest only. In some situations, refinancing your property can make sense rather than selling it to maximize your cash flow or return rate.

Tax Write-Offs-Tax write-offs can be a significant advantage of real estate investment for the right person. But sometimes they're not the panacea they're made to be. People who are hit by the Alternative Minimum Tax, who have many properties but they are not professionals in real estate, or who are not actively in their real estate investments may find cut off from some of the IRS tax sweetest breaks. Even worse, investors focusing on short-term real estate deals such as flips, rehabs, etc. have their income treated as EARNED INCOME. The short-term capital gains tax rate they pay is the same (high) they would pay if they earned income in the aW-2 job. After the Tax Reform Act burned down a lot of investors in the 1980s, a lot of people agreed that investing in real estate was a bad idea just for the tax breaks. They can be a high center of benefit if you qualify, but usually, you can find them the frosting on the cake, not the cake itself.

Any residential real estate investment deal that stands up under the scrutiny of this first lens should keep your real estate portfolio and your pocketbook healthy, whether the investment market for residential real estate is going up, down, or sideways. But if you can use the trends in the real estate market to give you a boost, it's also fair. The key is not to rely on any "strategy" to try to make outsize gains for you. Stick to the basics and be practical with your goals. You can afford to buy the property and plan to remain invested for the long haul.

Real Estate Internet Marketing

Most officials found marketing for real estate as a great way to highlight their business. The Internet has opened the world to a new person without whom many people wouldn't know existed. There are millions of companies that are currently based on their success on the internet.

It's relatively easy to start in real estate internet marketing as long as you have proper guidelines in place. It's up to you to know what properties you want to include on a forum and what other stipulations you wish to include in your post listing.

Internet real estate marketing can open the eyes of people to various properties around the world. Using online services means that people from all walks of life and different regions around the world can be attracted.

The world is moving too quickly, and in hopes of finding a home, many people don't have the time to look around to different locations. In reality, they leave a great deal of their decision on the internet. They choose to explore real estate sites until they find a home they are interested in. They will then be sufficiently intrigued to call the agency that corresponds to the house and ask a few more details about the home.

Real estate agents have made the use of this marketing technique unnecessarily simpler for their careers. Listing the property using a program such as a web 2.0 and allowing the calls to flow in is easy. They don't wait hopelessly for someone to be interested in what they're offering. Some agents have found social media sites that also allow them to reach buyers.

Thus with this new technique, the agents make a better profit than they have ever seen before. Their actual office time is significantly reduced. Because they're just too busy to stay in, they're showing off their homes, and the best of all closing deals.

By using this marketing method, agents can attract people from all over the world. They're not trapped in attracting people who live around the city mainly. It ensures that the city's overall economy in which the home is situated can also continue to flourish.

The recession has caused the industry a considerable strain. However, the real estate agency has been able to build itself up and avoid the avid job losses that started over the past year through this form of marketing.

The Off-Market Deals

Today, the real estate commercial market has been the competitive it in a long time. In addition to looking through listed business deals, you need to find non-listed off-market deals to give yourself the better opportunity and work effectively to succeed.

He has made 40 deals worth about $100 million over the past three years to give you an idea of a particularly successful real estate investor. Only ten of the forty offers were listed and promoted conventionally within that time frame. Of his 40 deals, thirty were off-market deals. By not looking for these off-market deals, you throw away a lot of great opportunities.

The point to have in the mind is that every individual can be a lead potentially. It would help if you also searched at smaller brokerages in addition to buying offers from major companies like Sperry Van Ness or CB Richard Ellis. Most people still run little brokerages that can work out of homes and have a low profile. Often these brokers can have great deals they may not have advertised or may have under-marketed the property as well.

Strategies that you can use to buy assets off-market. The first is the transaction that failed. This happens when a property has entered into a contract but has been unable due to the buyer's reasonable reasons. As a result, the seller may become very irritated. This is an excellent opportunity to quickly and efficiently jump in and purchase the land. To appease the seller, use short due diligence periods and possibly include a non-refundable deposit. Due to the speed and professionalism that you display through the deal, the seller may be willing to make concessions on price and other matters within the contract.

The second strategy you can use is to look at a particular market's largest owners. Check at these owners ' overall portfolios and see if there are assets that do not fit in with the portfolio's overall strategy. Such owners may not be used to maintain this land, and the form of return they will typically receive may not be obtained. Through taking over a part of their portfolio that they don't want or need, you will enter the picture and help them out. This will encourage the owner to get rid of a distressed property while providing you with an uncompetitive offer.

This on off-market deals should have given you an idea of why finding off-market sales is so critical along with two strategies. Off-market transactions are a source of deals that can't be ignored. You limit the amount of success you can have on the market if you choose to avoid this area. Hopefully, in the near future, you will be able to use this information in your business.

CHAPTER FOUR
How to Buy Real Estate Below Market Value

It requires time, work, and the ability to make a fantastic land deal. Obtaining a profitable transaction is one of the tasks of the whole business. But here we're going to let you know how to make a profit from buying a property. Doing this requires research, skillful transaction, and complete dedication-even if you follow the techniques given below, you can achieve amazing results.

You need to know how to buy land below the market value and buy properties that bode well to be effective in real estate. We'll let you know why individuals offer wealth below market value, what its actual market value is, and how you can buy land below market value afterward.

Why do individuals below market value offer the property?

No one wants to offer less than their value to their property. If you do that, there must undoubtedly be a reason for that. In most situations, time pressure is an explanation. In these situations, decisions can often be irrational and emotional.

For example,

- Facing budgetary issues,
- Swap the legatee's assets.
- Problems with foreclosure
- Interested in a different property.
- Migration due to job problems.

If you discover a dealer who is involved in Short Sale, it is nothing less than a golden opportunity for you to offer the deal in your favor with the terms of cost and contract.

In such situations, never hesitate to ask questions such as: "What is the reason for the sale?"; "How long has the property been available on the market?"; knowing such information will give you a clear understanding of how much space there is for negotiation, which will make your deal easy.

What's the real value of its market?

Market value is the original cost of selling a particular property in its present condition. The business sector calculates the expense, or sometimes it also depends on a buyer and dealer's relationship. Remember that at a retail store, it is not settled as the cost of an item. In an extraordinarily successful open door, this allows land bargains. There is only one way to find the precise estimate of a property in the business sector if you are not an agent, and that is by witnessing the same deals. Recent offers of comparable properties in surrounding areas need to be discovered for this. It's the most accurate way to do it alone. Likewise, for such service providers, the least complicated way to know the market value for this is to go. They will take full responsibility for providing you with an advantageous deal.

Remember, if you're looking at a property that requires repairs, you'll need to get it at even lower cost; otherwise, you're not buying on the real market value.

Approaches to buy real estate below market value: Most importantly, to purchase real estate, it becomes know that there are sales short below market value, Fair deals of market, auction property, and off-market properties can be sold below market value. Go for these properties with a specific end goal of using the benefits of buying real estate below its market value.

Short sales for financial specialists are a phenomenal hotspot. Private vendors own short sales; however, the vendor is committed to paying the bank more than the amount they try to offer the home. With a specific end goal of selling the house, the bank needs to consent to receive less cash than is due. Indeed, it takes up to 6 months or even a year to close short sales as sellers here don't hop to a conclusion. They take the time they need to settle for choice.

Fair deals market is claimed homes in the home selling decisions by a personal seller with reasonable play. Without including the bank in the necessary leadership, they should sell it. Because the dealer is not generally in a huge hurry to sell their home under market value, it is harder to discover fair market deals. On a fair market sale, there are fewer situations where you can find a lot.

Many service providers go for a property that is never listed for sale as they expect it might cost them not precisely the real market value, and they could quickly gain the advantage. These are off-market properties, as they are not available for purchase. It requires cash and investment to be able to purchase these kinds of features of speculation.

When a seller dispossesses a property, it is, therefore, obligatory for him to try and reclaim his misfortunes before promptly assuming the property's responsibility. That property is called the property that has been auctioned. That's why many homes are unloaded at the steps of the courthouse. So you should decide when the local court conducts its auctions and compete with it as soon as possible with the most lucrative offer.

Furthermore, never let go of the deals in which the seller uses such terms:

- The merchant was desperate.
- Diminished Property
- Land in distress.

Generally speaking, induced seller to find out how to buy real estate below market value, all you need to do is do a lot of work and save time in testing, so your offer can be extremely profitable after adopting these techniques.

How to track an outlook Real Estate Joint Venture PARTNER?

Much attention is paid to finding money to make your real estate deals these days. But what if you're someone to invest with a little money? How do you know what a great deal is?

One of the simplest ways to invest in real estate when you have the cash to spend is to partner with someone with an excellent track record, to invest in the kind of deals that work for your interests, and to give you a product that makes sense for your money. But how are you going to find them? And how are you going to screen them to be sure they fit you and your hard-earned cash?

The best way to get prospective joint venture partners these days is to do an online search. Most of the people running an investment business have a website or blog that explains the types of deals they make and provides some kind of education and information. You could search for opportunities to invest in real estate and find someone local in your area.

But the best way to find someone with whom to invest is to go into a couple of club meetings that invest in your local real estate. You can question friends and family if they know someone invests in real estate successfully.

Once you have found a few different people, meet face to face with each of them. You invest as much, or more, as you are in the deal itself in the ability of the person to manage the transaction. You want to make sure you invest your money with checks out the person you are.

Ask yourself and your prospective partner, is this investment in line with my objectives? If you want to study real estate along the way, you may want to find a partner who can teach you and invest your money. If you really want to be hands-on with your deals, then you're going to look for someone to work with a hands-on partner and maybe give you a larger share of the agreement in exchange for your efforts. Or, if you get out of the whole thing, make sure that you find someone who can make the right decisions after turning over your money. You need to know what's most important to you - and then check that this prospective partner will fit your goals and the deals they're making.

What's your record of the track? Past performance does not always mean future success, but it can tell you a lot about someone how to answer this question. In six years, we have received more than 700 percent return on his investment from one of our investors. In five years, we also earned 110 percent of the same partner on another venture. Rarely state these examples to prospective partners because It wants to set expectations too high when much of the return was due to a fast-growing market. Instead, tell them not sure in anything, let real estate alone, they feel well comfortable recommending a return of 15-20 precent on most of the investments we make.

Hear how somebody addresses this question carefully. When they tell you about their best deals and don't mention the worst, dig into their bad deals to get a sense of how they've benefited from their past experiences. And to get a sense of how honest and open-minded they are. Look for a process of decision-making and the ability to take responsibility for bad deals. This is far more important than finding someone who once made a return of 700 percent on somebody's money.

How is your credit? Can I get your credit report copy? When you donate your money to someone to handle, you believe you have every right to consider how your prospective partner feels their own assets. If they can't even manage their own, you'd never trust someone else with your money. No one loves MY MONEY as much as you do. If someone else doesn't like their own money, how comfortable are they going to give you the attention and care they deserve?

Have your references? Ask to talk to one or two of the people they had previously worked with. If they never partnered with anybody, you could talk to coworkers present or past. Whether they treat themselves at work is an excellent example of how someone is going to handle themselves with their finances. If they were right decision-makers and got along well at the office with others, then there's a perfect chance that they'll get along well and make the right decisions about your deals.

It's an excellent start to these questions, but it's not enough. ALWAYS go and see for yourself the deal. It's not about guessing the expertise and experience of the person with whom you're working, and it's about covering your ass. Look at the property to identify work in the near future that may be needed. Walk the neighborhood to make sure that investing in it is a good market.

Finally, determine whether the property has alternative exit strategies. If the proposed approach is not working, there are other ways to get out of this deal.

Once you are satisfied with all of the above, you can feel comfortable and confident to move forward to discuss terms of the deal and possibly get into real estate with a partner of the joint venture.

How to Win Commercial Real Estate Listings More

You should create and give the fullest vision and interpretation of what you see when you look at a specific commercial property for the first time, for sale or for lease. This allows the client to relate to their ability and ability to assist them. You can see the client only once to a large extent, and this may be the only opportunity you have to impress them and close on the listing.

It's shocking how many commercial sales and leasing people perform, without much thought, most of the first inspection and interview process. The questions and dialog that they use come from the top of the head in many situations. The whole thing is quite ordinary professionally. In some cases, no wonder the company hires another agent.

It's elementary mathematics to win the ranking. Show you're the best and they're going to choose you. So how do you get to the recognition of this 'holy grail' of the industry? You have to be visibly better than the others, and you have to do this with the prospect at the meeting. Let the 'toolbox' support the process with your ideas and skills.

We all know that many agents use some type of proposals to show that they know what they are doing and that they are relevant to the appointment of the property. Unfortunately, most of the recommendations in the format are the same and say the same thing. Then the customer gets to make cheaper and low-cost decisions rather than great ideas. That's a foolish way to go when dealing with a value-added investment property.

How are you better at showing you?

In the client interview, this toolbox phase put me way ahead of the others and elevated sales to more listings and industry to a large extent. The' ' toolbox' was a series of specially designed forms and checklists that brought the client on the road to closing on the listing selectively.

Without this 'toolbox' process, the customer has only to compare agent with an agent and thus come back to decisions about the standard facts of

- Cost
- Commission rate
- Marketing costs
- Marketing strategies
- Agent success in the region

Regrettably, the customer then took charge of the listing interview with the agents and will seek to make all agents 'cave in' under pressure. Be proud of your unique services for commercial real estate, and make sure the customer sees you are the best for the job.

When the listing decision of the client comes down to who gives the most to close the listing in concessions, you'll feel you've 'won' the listing but 'lost' the advantage of a first listing appointment. You are going to accept a listing on the terms and conditions of the company and not your own. Probably from the point of disadvantage and not control, you will have to market the property. The likelihood of selling or leasing has diminished.

The toolbox approach is still a recommendation and uses on the market today, especially the market as we emerge from the global economic crisis.

It is clear that the toolbox approach still works very well, as most of your competitors are ordinary when it comes to listing presentations and have nothing special to offer. There's nothing to excite the customer about.

So what's the toolbox, and how do you build it on your own? You make and use checklists. Read on, please.

Here are some ideas to better when listing In the presence of the client, always do the inspection. Make sure that the company knows that your review procedures are comprehensive.

Description of the property's physical and other characteristics should be recorded during your review on standard well-designed forms so you can ask great questions and document the things that really matter. Those agents and salespeople who rely on random top issues of the mind are not as active as those who have proper forms of checklist type for the process.

Use tools such as a laser measuring device and a measuring wheel to put a bit of theater into your inspection.

Divide the checklists between the layout of the property and the location of the property.

Have a particular checklist for inspecting the tenancy areas and do so by tenant suite area if necessary on a tenant.

Use a dictaphone as you walk around to make verbal notes.

Take pictures to document critical processes and property aspects.

Identify critical questions about the sale or lease campaign that the customer has so that you can feed the answers as a Q and A format into your proposal.

First, visit the local Planning Office to see what planning and zoning issues might affect your property.

Look at the neighboring properties surrounding the subject property for relationships.

Look for the local area's environmental impact, such as streams, rivers, and hills.

Examine the road access to the main access points. Look at the property's parking availability Check out the property's services such as curbing, roads, electricity, water, communications, gas, and anything else a tenant would need to make the property work.

Where does the labor market come from, and do they need to get to the property by public transport?

Check out the other local businesses to get a sense of how the streets and neighborhoods work. Pay particular attention to things that frustrate local companies, such as peak times and events.

Look at the internals of the property and draw on the property's physical and positive qualities that will attract buyers or tenants. Try these now decide what the property's target market should be and how to get to the target market.

Real Estate Investor Marketing

Real estate investor marketing begins with marketing to sell deals of wholesale, find many contacts. To find investors in the area who are finding for houses to rehabilitate and resell, you should be marketing. Make sure to meet and network with other investors in your real estate local investors association. You can find out who is searching for what and who are the real investors.

Second, call anyone with bandit signs up and run ads in the paper. If they're searching for inspired buyers, they're basically looking for deals, so ask them what they're looking for. Tell them you're still shopping for sales, and sometimes at any given time, you get more than you can manage. Let them know that if you have something, you will contact them, likewise let them know that if they have something, they can contact you. Remember, the marketing of real estate investors begins with you making contacts. You should be marketing at all times!

If you have an internet presence, one of the things you can do is set up a squeeze page or an opt-in for investors to sign in. You will relay it to everybody when you have offered. If you haven't begun your online marketing to real estate investors, you're missing out on the new frontier!

Place a paper ad that says something about it, Attention Investors! Fixer upper special! Available at 70% off the price. Do not forget to add a contact number!

Once you have your list, create a flyer outlining the house with pictures, estimated cost of repair, and your evaluation of the comps, and expected gross profit.

You should have an empty list of customers battling for your offers if you've done your job up front! If you have the contract, don't start selling your real estate investor, you should be marketing upfront and making connections at all times. You never know when your next deal is going to fall into your lap!

INVESTOR MARKETING REAL ESTATE

Are you in line with your competition? Knowing what works for your game could move you to the front very much.

What are you going to do to do this?

The best way to do this is to network through the email list of everyone. If you're networking enough, investors selling properties are likely to receive 5-10 emails every day. Real estate investor selling you their goods from guru's attempt to sell you would not count as emails for networking.

Getting an email from a real estate investor selling you should be a chance to look over the content and see if there is a gem from which you can learn. What are they selling exactly? Is this really a good deal about your needs?

Let's look at an example: an investor is pretty sharp and closes a lot of wholesale deals. If unexpectedly, a swirl of transactions from a specific section of the city, know how to start marketing there. This is where you get to do your due diligence. Plus, if you know your marketing superior to the others, you will likely receive more calls from your pieces marketing than he did.

The inexperienced and uneducated investor who knows nothing about this business thinks it's a good deal to offer $180,000 on a $200,000 property. It's pretty good to format and arrange the emails they send out for their wholesale deals. Although no real substantial deals are shared by the information in the emails, they can still learn from them how to make offers.

The marketing of real estate investors is no different from any other company. If you want to stay on top, research the competition at all times.

It may not be wise to copy anything your competition does, but if you find something that works. Use this to the maximum!

Call bandit signs in your town, just to hear how they handled the pitch for you. They have always been listening to a voice mail on a regular basis, and you have not been impressed by what you have heard most of the time.

Rather than getting annoyed with all the emails in your inbox, start appreciating them, even if you don't want to buy a bulk offer. You never know what the email or direct mail bid of today will bring, and it might be a brainy idea that you will get from a fellow real estate investor.

Marketing, as in other companies, is the key to success. Whether we enjoy it or not, we have to market properties to buy and sell. Good marketing is all and makes a lot less of a fight to sell. It's funny, you don't have to be showy, and you don't even have to be an expert. For respectable real estate investor marketing, you just need to be out there. Many successful investors may know bandit signs work better, but they have been made more hard to use by regulation from many cities across the country. That's why it's so frustrating because it's one of the most effective marketing forms you can use and one of the least expensive.

REAL ESTATE WHOLESALING MARKETING FUTURE

What is the future of real estate investor wholesaling marketing?

It's nice to know what's working right now. However, as clearly seen from recent business fights over the course of history between Apple and Google and real estate companies, it is those who embrace future trends and stay at the forefront of change who continually sprint ahead and remain at the top.

In simple wholesale marketing strategies such as bandit signs, direct mail, and, personal networking, of course, online content marketing many consumers are currently finding great success.

While many of those reading this could instantly be crying, expecting this to be yet another of the same old pieces you've got to use social and mobile parts, that's not necessarily the only future of wholesaling.

As with the economy and the housing market, all marketing is cyclical. The print has gone out and returned, so you've got direct mail and email marketing. In the early 2000s, all of them were very popular and successful, then died off and were revived. So some of the more traditional advertising strategies would definitely have scope for rebounding in the future, even if they take on a much more digital format.

Obviously, however, technology cannot be ignored either. Even if we don't want to be, we are all increasingly being wired in. Wholesale marketing offline may continue for quite some time to produce real estate leads and offers for flipping houses, but investors will have to adjust at some point. You can put it off and lead your competition or start strategizing now to get the edge and enjoy market dominance and more lead flow.

Mobile is a clear trend. bulk SMS, Apps, responsive mobile sites, and social are best ways for free movement to capitalize. It, however, would definitely also mean sensitive digital outdoor ads, social alerts on smartphones, in the car, and through Google Glass, based on all kinds of location and activities, also with no prospects asking for it.

It is not possible to ignore the psychological. Some may have not yet figured out how to use it effectively, but that doesn't mean that if done right, it's not incredibly valuable or powerful and high ROI. Social, in fact, is just figuring out itself. Once properly marketed and wholesalers are able to infiltrate feeds, they can be monetized by offering timed messages and valuable info. The focus should, meanwhile, be on building a tight customer tribe and being genuinely authentic.

Looking For Discounted Real Estate Deals

Have you ever been frustrated with finding your next deal from your latest search and concluded that there are no excellent property deals out there? This opinion has been shared by many real estate entrepreneurs from time to time. In reality, it couldn't be further from the facts. You can be sure that there are deals out there regardless of what, no matter when. If you don't find any contracts, you may need to sharpen your tactics, or your sights may need to widen.

Searching for a property can be a time-consuming operation, resulting in many investors relying too heavily on their realtors to locate their assets. While many realtors do a great job of finding a suitable investment property, they are often limited to features on the MLS.

There are a lot of origin deals techniques that allow you to bypass the realtor and deal with the seller or owner specifically, in which you can find several of the best deals.

The process of dealing directly with an owner can be much more fruitful as you have the opportunity to make the sales process more relationship-based than represented or operated through a realtor. Remember, people are doing business with people they like in sales. It's no different to find and negotiate a great real estate deal. It's all about sales and your sales process.

The opportunity to ask your own questions in order to discover the underlying motive behind the sale allows you to become empathic with their position, which can produce the best platform for a win or win the always deal.

There are many ways to find the right deals; the challenge is to get out and pound the pavement itself for many investors who rely exclusively on their realtors. So what is the nature of pavement pounding?

Here are ways to make deals with the forest. They are not in any order of preference or effectiveness.

- Owner's Call for Purchase (FSBOs).

Through reviewing For Sale through Owner advertising from a major local magazine, a small neighborhood newspaper, or online ads, you can find owners. We are generally found in the category of Houses for Sale. There are keywords to check for which the degree of seller motivation may be predictive.

Second, there are many "For Sale by Owner" companies that offer their clients who sell their homes discount flat rates. These firms provide pictures and property details to a website as well as owners ' contact information. This allows you to contact the owners and start your own sales process directly.

- Call the ads for rent.

There are a lot of landlords out there who no longer want to be landlords. Many have no time, money, or patience in dealing with tenants, property management, or maintenance. You can get a friendly owner on the phone by calling rental ads that may be more than willing to negotiate. Some people may need to sell, but they didn't have the time or energy to sell the property until you called them. Timing can be all it takes to find a lot.

- Drive the districts.

Potential deals could be within walking distance. Choose an area of about 300 homes. Become an expert in the field. Check for signs of distress and drive the area regularly. Such symptoms can be something like:

- Mail collecting for weeks or months at the front door
- Excessive house decay
- Overgrown lawn, hedges, and landscaping
- door lockers, railings, or poles
- Boarded windows in the basement
- Zoning or public notices placed on windows or doors
- Clutching at the window.

Go up to the door and knock at the door when you see the property in the condition described above. What are you going to say? Something like, "Hi, your name is, you're an investor in real estate, and you're interested in buying a neighborhood house, and you're just knocking on the doors to see if anyone is interested in selling." Once you've ended your talk, go to other neighbors, and do the same. Use the main 10-10-20. That's ten houses on the left, ten on the right and 20 on the other side of the street.

You build your presence with other neighbors by doing this, and you may find a sale where you least expect.

- Put on the doors notices or letters.

Similar to the above suggestion (or if there is no one home), you can post notes or letters to a property's door that seems to be in a troubled state. There are many ways to write such a note or message, but it can be as easy as "Hi to owner of the house. My name is, and you I like to buy your house. Please call me if you are interested." Go to your local board of Landlord or Tenant.

There are proceedings that are held at landlord or tenant boards across the country on a regular basis. These are happening by a mediator both in the courtroom and outside the courtroom. Attending these hearings from day to day gives you the opportunity to meet with landlords or property managers who have just come from an experience they may not have had to go through. They may be very willing to discuss the sale of their property with you.

- Go to the court of the foreclosure.

It can be an exciting experience to go to the foreclosure court. You can witness hearings of foreclosure that will be in their processes at different stages. The owners are sometimes present and sometimes not. The reason for attending, other than for building up yourself, is to meet likely owners and be able to help them. This may include financial assistance, advice to save the house, or an offer to purchase the property. It can be invaluable for them to offer excellent options to owners who are unfamiliar with the process. Comprehend the process of foreclosure in your province.

- Ads are placed.

To get your message out, use local papers and online ads. Simple words like, "I can buy your house quickly!" "Do you need to sell your house today?" It can be as simple as "you buy houses." These ads work well under the section called "Money to Lend" and attract people who are looking for cash to keep their houses. They may read your advertisement and realize it can ease their financial pressures if they just sold their house.

- Realtors contact.

You are creating a simple message. "I'm looking for distressed apartments in your area of selection that can get under market price for at least 10 percent (or whatever the number is). You can buy cash and close quickly." If you fax this to all local real estate brokerages, you should get calls. This can be the initiation to create some great relationships with realtors who can find some great deals for you.

- That's right. Mouth word.

No better advertising is available to you than word of mouth. Just like in any kind of sales, when a trusted friend, neighbor, or business partner pass your name to someone they feel can benefit from what you're doing, it comes as an excellent recommendation for the person who receives it. As your service and credibility may have already been addressed, this can help dramatically in your sales process. All you can do now is to fill in the need and sell.

When it comes to choosing more offers, it is not the lack of resources that keeps real estate investors from achieving their investment goals, but rather the lack of resourcefulness.

Real Estate Deals That Are Under Market Value by Networking

Every successful investor is passionate about their business and can't wait to talk about it to people. Nonetheless, to maximize positive response, there must be a framework for your efforts. So what's marketing on the network anyway? For purposes beyond the reason for the initial contact, network marketing establishes business relationships. These relationships can lead through a referral to more business directly or indirectly. Networking is a very positive marketing tool. The establishment and maintenance of relations require a daily commitment. It's no different from your personal life. To make them successful, you must continuously work on relationships. The greatest mistake investors make, first of all, focusing on themselves and their own needs. Understand that when you help others is the safest way to help yourself, you're bound to benefit from networking with different groups of people.

1: Knowledge Why Investors Need To Network Market

Networking is one of the critical components of a well-designed marketing campaign. The reason why networking can be such an effective avenue is that you can identify the business with a face and a personality. This is where the world makes all the difference to your charisma. People like to work with people they know, and they love it. Have your best attributes shine, therefore, and establish a level of confidence. The primary way to do this is to show genuine interest in people-who they are and what they are doing. The overall goal of networking is to promote the business and educate as many people as possible about the services your company offers. Broader exposure often leads to new opportunities, prospective customers, and new ideas, and there is no better way of achieving this goal than by networking.

Opportunities for networking are genuinely endless and limited by your imagination and willingness to interact with people around you. There's virtually no one you get in touch with that you shouldn't be aware of what you're doing and what services you have to offer. One of the great things about real estate investment is that it naturally involves all kinds of social, economic, and professional backgrounds. The shelter is one of the core human needs, so you shouldn't have trouble starting a real estate discussion and finding common ground for a conversation. Whether you're a prospective home seller, real estate investor, private lender, buyer, or a renter, you should let all of them know business you are doing and how to serve them. All these connections are a valuable property for your company. If you get advantage of the opportunities provided by networking, also they can be a significant source of revenue for your business. You will find that most of the time, in your close social circles, you offer a service that is sought after among the people.

2: Best places to look at networking

The local Real Estate Investors Association is the first starting point networking. You can find dozens, if not hundreds, of-minded investors with specific experience levels at your local REIA. Whether you are looking to buy or sell, this is your market.

The local home builder's association and apartment owners association is another great place to network. The association of home builders is a different type of association, the membership of which usually consists of builders and suppliers. In case you get into real estate development or serious remodeling work, these friendships will be precious. Local landlord associations can also be of great value for your multi-unit properties and a great source of wholesale buyers.

There are also specially organized events for networking purposes. They are a great way to meet other professionals working in fields related to real estate and non-immobilities. It's a very efficient way to create new relationships because everyone has the same agenda, which is to make as many contacts as possible that can benefit their business. It's like going to a bar for singles, where there's everyone to mix. This eliminates any uncomfortable about getting right down to business. For your marketing campaigns, you will meet many people who will be valuable assets. We met with reps from ad agencies, media buyers, printers, and a lot of private lenders at different networking events.

3: How to Network Effectively

Don't miss this part of the course, thinking it's not necessary, and you already know how to meet people and network effectively, but it's not an environment you want to neglect. Not that easy for everyone to become a charismatic person that individual want and like to do business partner with. It's requires effort and practice.

Rapid reporting is something you need to do when you're networking. Next, find out about the other person as much as you can and let them make most of the initial conversation. Next, ask them questions that were open to get them to talk. People enjoy talking about themselves. It's funny, but the more people you listen to, the more they love you and respect you. You will give them a little two to three minute talk about your business after finding out about them as much as possible and how it can be of service to them. People always want to know how to help them to let them know. If you take the initiative and introduce them to someone they'd like to know or help them in some way, they'll be grateful to you forever. Whenever you take time to help a new investor, you will find that the generosity will be returned in deals that they will bring to you many times over.

Do not try to connect with the entire room. You should try to connect with just three or four new people when you attend a networking event and find a reason to follow up with them. It is the aspect of follow-up that usually leads to opportunities for you as an investor in real estate.

CHAPTER FIVE
Real Estate Mistakes to Avoid

There are some things to consider and understand ahead of time before taking the plunge into the real estate market. With laws, fees, and rules continually changing, most people seem lost when it comes to buying. It would result in a very long list to list any mistake people make while buying. Instead, here are some mistakes people make when they either buy the property or get a mortgage.

The first mistake is that the customer does not understand the new ways to buy and sell the property. While the basics of finding funding, shopping for a home, making an offer, and then closing are almost the same, the finer details of how the process works today are different from last year. Knowing the new rules and knowing what has changed is essential to prevent any costly errors.

Homebuyers pay more for land than they should be, a common problem in real estate purchases. Although this is a market for buyers, it is essential you do your research and familiarize yourself with home prices in the areas that you are considering buying in. It is also crucial not to allow your purchase decision to be distorted by the fear of' missing out.' Prices of property can go down as fast as they go up. Unless you're ready, don't be pressured into buying. Jumping to the first property is another common mistake for new home buyers. Even if you're in love with the first house, you're visiting, and you still need to take the time to look around. While the home is beautiful, you may find that the next one has a finished basement or more bedrooms at a more reasonable price.

Lenders are now asking for much more documentation than they did six months ago, so be prepared to provide extensive documentation with your application and during the verification process when you apply for a mortgage. Not responding to the requests for verification documents from your bank or lender will only delay the process, which may result in declining funding, which could cause you to miss a lot. Cleaning up your score is one of the most important factors to consider when you spend or buy — very tightened credit standards for borrowers. Before, a loan with a lower score could be obtained. Nevertheless, to get a loan, government-backed loans now need a minimum credit score of 600. Before applying for a loan, you must cleaning spend time up your credit score.

It has been said that those who are not learning from history are condemned to repeat it. With the real estate market in a downward cycle, it's an excellent time to go over some of the more popular "no - no's." Here are my picks for mistakes to avoid-TRYING TO PICK THE TURNS Most sellers and buyers play this game, trying to time there selling or purchase, get to the top of the market and receive optimum income, or swoop in and pluck up the cheap property after a blast. This is a year when the exchange of the seller has become the market of a buyer, and prices have eased. But there is an uneven spread of the slowdown across the country. But there has been a sudden "ring" nowhere, and you should certainly not expect one. Historically, for the most part, real estate bubbles don't pop up, they're only slowly deflating, and then the level of the market is rising again.

Please take the approach of a long-term investment in real estate.

You know what happens when you make choices based on optimism, time-on - the-market averages, and optimistic agent commitments— you old Murphy's law kicks in. The process of home selling is often more drawn out than you think, from early planning to financial arrangements, too tricky negotiations, to final inspections, to frequently delayed closures. Give yourself extra time to finish the deal.

Try to contain your enthusiasm for the house that you are planning to buy, otherwise, it will cost you money. When you get back in your car, you can scream, yes

Theoretically, evaluations represent objective value views. But emotion and self-interest can play a role, so ask your agent for several figures, an optimistic one, and a pessimistic one — a job with the negative.

Locate Potential Commercial Real Estate Deals

The essential element of commercial real estate investment can be to locate potential commercial real estate deals. In fact, you don't have any property to invest in without reliable deals. It is indispensable to find the best deals you can in order to maximize the return on your invested capital.

You can make bigger deals per year if you locate only great deals and make an exorbitant amount of money. Amazing deals are characterized by a return equal to three or four times your investment amount. When you only find average deals, however, the performance per transaction can be significantly lower, causing you just not to spend as much money or to make more deals per year. It takes for each deal the same amount of work and the same processes, so you could do less work and see a higher return as well.

To find your offers, you need to use reliable and trustworthy tools. Although there are many possibilities to find properties, as they are available in each city and state, with updated and accurate information, you must use resources. Below are the best resources to help you find deals. You can use every resource to locate the properties that fit your investment criteria for your property. Some resources, depending on your area of specialization, may work better than others.

Commercial brokers are one of the best and most common places to find a commercial property. This would make sense because they are the ones who have mentioned the property. With a criteria sheet or specific information about the type of property you want to buy, you can go to them.

Brokers can be found on a local or more widespread basis, even going as far as in other states calling brokers. Most will be glad to call other brokers and find listings that suit your requirements best. As they become available, they will bring you properties.

The significant advantage of a business broker is its ability to find pocket listings or listings that are about to be put on the market but have not yet been officially listed. You can make a leap in front of the competition and find great offers. Get in touch every day with a few brokers and see targeted properties roll in!

Another place is on the internet to find a property. Many locations where hundreds properties of commercial are available for sale interval from raw land to big retail and residential complexes. Such pages have both the property and the broker information so you can quickly get in contact with the broker and find out more about the house. Generally, according to your specific criteria, you can filter the details as you see fit.

This site is home to hundreds of brokers across the U.S. sharing their many listings. You can very rapidly filter by deals and reach a wider audience than you would in your own community. With several brokers and agents at your fingertips, your ability to build contacts also increases.

Auction houses are great places where all conditions and types of properties can be located. Many times you can get great property offers that you might otherwise have to spend a lot more on if they were listed with a broker. You can also get sending an e-mail lists of various auction houses so they will notify you of the properties to be auctioned. This allows you to moment before the actual bidding day to investigate the property as an investment.

Sellers sometimes offer the option of buying a property at a specific price before it goes to the auction. You never understand what opportunities will come along, so staying in touch with several auction houses is a good idea to be deprived of the properties that move through their hands.

Even though there are many ways to locate deals, they are among the best that the commercial real estate industry has to offer. The characteristics are abundant, and contacts can be continuously made so that other possible deals can easily be made. A secret in this business is that the more connections you have for you; the more opportunities you will see.

Use these other choices if you work locally and only use local resources such as lists, newsletters, and magazines. This way, you can also find local offers. You may even be encouraged to move out to your comfort zone and to places where you will find even more opportunities.

Use these resources-brokers, internet commercial real estate pages, and auction houses to find targeted, up-to-date, and numerous properties that might bring your next big business deal!

Avoid Mistakes When Making Money in Real Estate

In the art of flipping, the highest profits can be found when it comes to making money in real estate. Flipping real estate is the process of purchasing a desirable fixer home, doing the work needed, and reselling it for a substantial profit. But while in flipping real estate, there are significant profits to be made, there is also a high potential for failure.

making money key in real estate is maximizing gains and reducing losses; both can be achieved by avoiding these mistakes most frequently caused by real estate investors: purchasing overpriced homes-making money in real estate involves buying a home significantly below value so that you can resell it at a much higher price. You'll have a hard time selling it for profit if you buy a home that's only slightly below market value. Remember, you also need to have adjustments to the budget, legal fees, broker commissions, taxes, operating costs, and leave room for unexpected expenses. All of these can have a dramatic impact on your bottom line, as you can imagine.

Buying properties that require too much work (for your individual experience)-While making money through estate flips always involves some remodeling or repair work, you can buy properties that have gone too far to build a profitable flip possible. Have better idea all time of how much the job you need will cost before you buy a home.

Not doing a title search-a title search will be done for you if you buy property by traditional means. But if you're buying foreclosed homes, it may be up to you to search your title. Never underestimate the need for a hunt for the word. Keep in mind that when you buy it, you will inherit all legal issues and ties related to a house.

Sticking to Schedule-Making money in real estate is only possible when you quickly buy and sell a house. You will have to pay interest charges and bank loans if you hold a property for too long. Make sure all of your building stays on schedule to avoid these expensive charges.

Gaining money in real estate sometimes has less to do with the smart choices you make and more to do with avoiding the costly mistakes that can cut your profits. For potential losses keeping your eyes open and will ensure that where it belongs, you keep your hard-earned profit.

The Things to Negotiate a Great Real Estate Deal

So quickly, it can happen If a property is from a distance, you can analyze it so quickly. You can easily see what kind of price makes sense to you, and what makes a lot.

Your competitive instincts then tend to kick in the second you plan to put in an offer.

As a property buyer looking at land, being rational about a property is so easy until you're in the midst of negotiating the contract.

Many people say that they would rather be wealthy than mediocre, but they live as if they were right rather than evil.

We draw a line in the sand and allow the other party to cross that line to make the deal. They pretend they're looking for the' win-win' scenario, but they're just thinking about winning.

You want to beat the vendor to give you the lowest possible price. At least you feel that way until you find out there's a competitive bid, and then you suddenly find yourself offering way beyond what you planned to offer just because you've got to win the deal.

Okay, I'm not going to pretend to be able to negotiate everything expertly - but years of sales work (from packaged goods to real estate information), training sales staff, and negotiating real estate deals have taught me a lot about what works and what doesn't.

Comfortable to hold it Here are the Great Real Estate Deals Commands for Negotiations:

- The only reason you're in a negotiation is to do better than your alternatives, so instead of winning make that your focus. Just last week, a fellow selling a rice alternative initially turned down an offer in return for knowledge and cash for 50 percent of his company that he badly needed. He had no other options. His other choice was to move away from his company. He said almost no because he felt that 50% was too high. But he's got 100 percent of a loss of $100,000 right now, and this deal would give him the chance to have 50 percent of the business of $5,000,000 a year. He would have lost sight of being there to do better than his alternatives would not feel like the king of Canadian national television negotiations.
- Be a solution to the problem. Why is the selling person? Ask many questions in order to try and understand the seller's motivation. Then find out how you can solve your problem in the best way. Maybe the seller needs their full purchase price to close more quickly than they need. If you work on answering the seller's question, you won't know what kind of deal you can make.
- BC Lottery Corporation's line to steal: Know your limit, play within it. In other words, BEFORE you set your foot in a negotiation, determine what you think is a good deal. And that's going to be a choice, not a number. Take the sale if you receive any amount within your range. Resist the urge for the last $2,000 to squeeze.
- Remember, when negotiating a prominent real estate deal, it's not just about price. Have a limit on what you're going to pay, but find other ways to get the deal to work for you and the seller. For example, if the vendor is going to finance the property, you will often find that you can get the deal done with less trouble and fewer expenses.
- Be versatile and not angry. The buying price range is a good thing to have, but if you find other ways to make the deal work for every-

one, you may choose to bend it. The trick is to analyze the deal without becoming emotional. If you start feeling too nervous about taking a step back at any time, review the deal's numbers and facts. What's a good deal for you?

- Options= Strength. Talk about your choices when you start feeling like you're getting back into a corner. Even better, if you don't make this deal, think about your best option before you even start. The founder of Good to Great, Jim Collins, terms it a BATNA-the best alternative to a negotiated agreement. As you think about your options, you know that there are going to be other offers, and no matter how much you like this property, it's never worth overpaying for a property just to get it.

- Options= Seller control as well! Rather than being a hard-nosed negotiator forcing the seller to agree to your offer, try to make decisions for the seller. If you make the seller feel like they have some power and control over the deal, you have a better chance to understand their problem and get the deal you want. For instance, to keep from having the dealer say "no" to your offer, say anything like this: "The easiest I can do is $200,000 if you have to go to a bank for funding. They're going to require you to prove the rental income, pay for an assessment, and do a ton of paperwork to qualify for that loan. So if you're going to accept the $200,000 offer, you're going to close on the date you want even if one of them would be a lot for you.

- It says no to a confused mind. It is quite right. When were you lost and decided to do something? It's just not true. Explain your offer so merely that it would understand your 8-year-old niece. And if you rely on your realtor to inform the realtor of the seller and then the realtor of the seller to explain it to the seller should consider writing a letter with the bid to be made. Explain what you are offering and why in the message. Keep it simple and targeted.

- Explain the reason. Determined that even a bad excuse is far more critical than no reason at all. In a line-up of people waiting to make copies, he studied this. When someone asked to go to the front of the line, most people turned them down but when they asked and included "because you're in a hurry" or "because you've got to make a couple of copies quickly"-that's really no reason at all, most people let that person in line before them! So be sure to provide a reason for the offer when you're making an offer. Explain why you bid less than market value and why you need a specific time frame. You don't have to show all of your cards, but you should give every opportunity to accept your deal to the seller.

- That's right. Negotiating is neither a game nor a sport. Negotiation is not a winning thing. It's really more of a science or an art. It's something that's very specific, but it's also something that's central to any agreement with principals. And it's something you can't judge by winning or losing, but the results can decide that. Do not let your negotiation turn into a game or a sport, and you will find that you are less likely to try to be right, which means that you are much more likely to be rich!

You will find the desired outcome in every real estate deal. If you keep in mind these commandments, you will always remember that you have choices and only make deals that make sense to you and your goals. This Negotiating not about winning, but winning. To an end, it's a means. Negotiations are literally a chance to do better than the alternatives. If you've got excellent options, you're going to do a lot because you have options, and options are giving you the power!

CONCLUSION

Buying property with nothing sounds like a lot and a perfect deal. After all, most people remain out from under clearly ignore the real estate market as an investment option Because they do not have the requisite big down payments for investment or private ownership properties

When you reach the real estate market as a down payment with little or no money because you don't have the cash and with the intention of flipping the house for a quick profit, think again. Over the past few years, mortgage firms who provided real estate with nothing down offers have discovered that sometimes when a person is unable to make a down payment, this is a warning sign of their ability to continue on the road with mortgage payments. Many borrowers have followed suit, and many properties with nothing down deals have dried up lately, or lenders are returning to the tradition of requiring at least a small percentage to pay down.

There are two specific forms of zero-down transactions. The first is offered by homeowners or property investors who do not have a mortgage on the property and who own the property directly. Owner financing is commonly referred to like this type of deal. The interest rate on loans is usually much higher than a conventional mortgage is affordable. This can be as much higher than average on three occasions.

You're investing several thousand dollars repairing the house and several thousand more apothecary dollars trying to sell the house just to find it doesn't sell in a reasonable time. Now you're out of luck, and the house is owned by the original owner. This is good for him because, for a short period of time, he had a good return on his investment, and some free work was done on his home. Miserable for you, you've lost thousands of dollars, and your credit rating is weak now.

The second type of zero down payment for investment in real estate is where the homeowner has a mortgage. Some of the Real Estate Gurus recommend this is the ideal type of opportunity for investment. You find a homeowner in financial distress and make a deal without notifying the mortgage company to take over the mortgage payments. While assuming mortgage payments is not illegal without notifying the holder of the underlying mortgage, it is a morally questionable practice.

Nearly all lenders have a clause in the contract that if the homeowner sells or transfers home title to someone else in some way, the mortgage underlying is payable on appeal. While the mortgage company can look the other way as long as the payments are kept up-to-date, they are not allowed to do so.

As for developers, the excitement and hysteria of property ownership are so easy to get caught up in. The population grew at such an incredible pace, and more and more people were buying homes that with any type of real estate investment, it seemed that you could do no wrong. Yet sadly, those who entered the real estate market because it was so easy to invest with nothing down in real estate find the bubble bursting now. For months and even years, properties are being sold and languishing on the market, with many also removing their homes from property listings. So while buying a property with nothing down at the time seemed like a good investment, many learn that down payment was just a small part of the decision process in buying or investing in property. Needless to say, buying real estate with nothing down is no guarantee that it will increase its value or that one could even sell it if the valuation went up.

And when it comes to real estate with nothing down deals, there's another reason to be careful. You might want to ask yourself why the individual sells the property at such a low price or in the first place without such requirements. If they don't want the property anymore, is there a justification for that? How is the local economy? What is rising or falling real estate prices and values? Sometimes it's just a warning sign in itself that someone offers real estate with nothing down.

It does not, of course, mean that all real estate deals without anything down are frauds and, therefore, should be avoided. It merely means that an investor or buyer should exercise extreme caution, do some schoolwork, and make this decision carefully.

There are eight steps in each real estate deal. These steps are to find the deals, initial review, make the decision, negotiate, inspect, close the deal, improve, and resell. For those of you who would like to delve deeper into this topic, these measures are listed below.

The first step of the acquisition cycle is the discovery of potential deals. Not only must these properties be great deals, but they must be personalized to your needs. You're looking for possible deals during this phase, doing whatever you need to find what you're looking for. This may include attending auctions, reading the paper on a daily basis, taking long drives in areas that interest you, or other search forms. Once you've seen a property you're interested in, go to step two.

You can do an initial property analysis in a matter of a couple of days or less. First of all, you have to look inside and out at the property itself, but you have to do some preliminary research on the property and the neighborhood. You must meet the neighborhood sellers, talk to neighbors, and find neighborhood property values to make sure you get the deal you expected at the start.

Create your own mind. For a potential investor, this is the hardest part. You now have to make the decision to purchase the property and take it as your new baby or hand it over and maybe allow some other real estate investor to benefit or lose on it. Take some time to write down and weigh each positive and each negative against each other to help you make this critical decision. If you find the pros outweigh the disadvantages, then it's time to start negotiations with the seller.

Negotiations are essential for investment in real estate. You want to know you're getting a lot, but you don't want the seller to think they're getting a lot of the raw end. Negotiations generally involve multiple offers and counteroffers, so don't be discouraged after shooting down your first bid.

Once you've agreed to a selling price, it's all written down, and the deal begins to close.

Before a mortgage can be issued, a professional inspection is required in most states. The examination is recommended, even if it is not needed, and you plan to pay cash for the land. You need to make sure the property is in good shape, and you won't have to do thousands of dollars' worth of maintenance that you couldn't spot when you first checked.

If the qualified review is all right and you've decided on a purchase price, it's time to sign or seal the papers. The house is yours after closing, and you can start the next move, improvements or renovations.

If you're known as the handyman family, you may find it easy to renovate. Typically, when you buy a home for profit, more work is needed than just cleaning and painting. If you're running into something you're not sure how to fix, calling a professional is best. If you're doing something you're unfamiliar with, you're probably going to cost more money than you're going to make on that part of the project. It's time for the best part, the resell, once the renovations are completed.

It is best to have a professional involved when it comes to selling the property. Someone who is unaware of the process might think selling a home is as easy as selling a car, but it's not as easy as you might think. Selling a home requires mountains of paperwork to be collected in the proper county and city departments, tax offices, and numerous other offices that you may not even know exist. Comparison shop around and make sure that in its current location, you don't ask too much for the home and go on selling!